THAT
POWERFUL
LIGHT

The story of
HERMANO
PABLO

LINDA FINKENBINDER

Printed in the United States of America
by Lightning Source Inc.
Cover design by Dennis Davidson

Library of Congress Control Number: 2011926939
ISBN: 978-1-61315-003-0

CrossHouse Publishing
PO Box 461592
Garland, TX 75046
1-877-212-0933

www.crosshousepublishing.org

Unless otherwise indicated, all Scripture taken from the Holy Bible,
New International Version, copyright 1973, 1978, 1984
by International Bible Society

Foreword

On a dark and drizzly night in Lima, Peru, I was driving with Hermano Pablo to a meeting in the center of the city. The light rain made it difficult to see ahead. Unfortunately, I went through a red light. We heard the police whistle, and soon saw the officer's face at the driver's side window! He started to tell me of my "very serious" infraction of the law, when he leaned in and saw my passenger. "Oh, pardon me" he said, looking at my front seat companion, "Aren't you Hermano Pablo?"—to which Paul said "Para servirle" (at your service). Without another word, the officer whisked us on our way!

Paul Finkenbinder, better known as Hermano Pablo, has been called the "Billy Graham of Latin America." He is, without doubt, the best-known and most loved evangelist in the Spanish-speaking world. He is by far the most genuine and transparent man I have ever known. It has been my joy to work alongside this unique servant of Christ for more than 40 years. The countless church and civic leaders who point to him as the model of true Christianity distinguish his life and service. He is a servant "in whom there is no guile."

His life and ministry, covering five decades, parallel the remarkable advance of the Gospel throughout Latin America. His radio program, "A Message to the Conscience" is heard 6,000 times daily in more than 33 countries from Mexico to Argentina, and throughout the Caribbean region. The Television version of the popular program has been added, and so today, thousands of Latinos hear a clear presentation of the Gospel message on their local TV stations.

Rev. Norman Mydske
Director of Ministries of the
Billy Graham Association

It is an extremely interesting study to see how God has used men and women down through the centuries in the building of His Church, starting with Jesus and His disciples and then going on through the Book of Acts with the apostles Jesus chose who were so greatly used in spreading the message of Jesus Christ beyond the borders of Jerusalem and into the known world. This group of men and women who were not highly qualified by human standards through God's help changed their world. They brought the Roman Empire to its knees as the claims of Jesus Christ were taken to the confines of the empire and even beyond.

In our lifetime, God has used men and women in very unique and special ways. The subject of this book is one of those special individuals God raised up with unusual talent and passion for His work, a man who is creative and full of faith, who was willing to launch out beyond the ordinary way of preaching the gospel and had the unique background and cultural settings to make him effective in his day.

He started out as a missionary in El Salvador at an early age and developed a love for the Salvadoran people and for the ministry God gave him during those early years-traipsing across the country on mule-back and other means to take gospel to this little land in Central America. But it wasn't long before God began to stir his heart with great and unusual ways of presenting the gospel way beyond the mule-back experience and to reach thousands through radio and TV. This ministry carried him beyond the borders of El Salvador throughout the entire Spanish-speaking world including other countries where Spanish-speaking people request the program.

I've had the honor of working closely with Paul and Linda from the beginning of our own ministry in El Salvador. I was able to capture firsthand the uniqueness of Paul's passion and creative spirit in serving his Master. Lois and I lived in their home for weeks at a time, and we were able to observe close up the greatness of this couple as they served the Lord.

I believe it is uniquely appropriate that Linda felt it in her heart to put in print some of the great experiences they have been blessed with down through the years and the influence and impact they've had on the lives of so many others. I don't know of anyone in my generation who has had more impact on reaching men and women for Jesus Christ, sometimes through a low-key approach to the experiences of life, to bring people into a search for the Master and for the blessings of Jesus in their life.

I am honored to be a friend of the Paul and Linda Finkenbinder and now to present this great work that is a labor of love of Paul's beautiful and faithful wife, who has shared with him the many experiences of life in El Salvador and around the world.

L. John Bueno
Executive Director
Assemblies of God World Missions

Table of Contents

Preface

Who is this legendary individual called Hermano Pablo? The activity and events of his dedicated life left an indelible mark of respect in the Hispanic world. However, only vague memories of this vivacious, ambitious, man of God, whose words stirred and continues to speak to the minds and hearts of millions of people through his "Message to the Conscience" program, remain.

During prayer in June 2007, I felt strongly impressed to chronicle the main activities of Paul's life. Each related incident describes a bit of the character and philosophy of this Godly man whose life I have shared for almost seven decades.

Ed Martinez was the first friend who encouraged me to write this account of my husband Paul, a man that I truly honor for his life-long commitment to God. My sincere gratitude goes to Ed and countless others whose valuable advice and counsel encouraged me to complete the narrative.

My desire is that the examples of the life of the Hermano Pablo you see and hear on radio and television and the Internet will inspire you as you travel life's journey and add to the exploits of the Apostles who went everywhere proclaiming the Gospel of our Lord Jesus Christ.

Linda Finkenbinder

Introduction
Spiritual Darkness

Paul and I were 22 years of age when we left our North America homeland in November 1943, with our 14-month-old son, Paul. We began missionary work in El Salvador, a republic 100 miles by 60 miles at its widest, boasting a population, at that time, of 2.5 million people.

At the beginning of our work, we were under the leadership of Ralph Williams and Melvin Hodges. The Williams' had been in that small republic since the end of 1929. With great sacrifices, they had established 26 churches that might possibly have had 1,000 members. In addition, they had established a Bible School where students studied for four months each year. Although the Baptists and other small groups had been ministering in El Salvador since the beginning of the century, the number of believers was quite insignificant.

Missionary life for us was novel in many ways. It rained for six months of the year, and the people cooked on clay stoves built against the kitchen wall. The smoke of the burning wood glazed the wall and ceiling a shiny black. Cement tanks of varying sizes held our supply of water, a precious commodity. The typical diet consisted of red or black beans, fried rice, thick handmade corn tortillas, semi-hard cheese, and tropical fruits.

According to local reports, 14 families "owned" El Salvador, and most of the country's citizens earned their living by working in the coffee and sugar cane plantations, which were the principle exports of the country. This noticeable disparity of wealth made a middle-class society almost extinct in the country where we now lived.

El Salvador's constitution guaranteed religious liberty; however, the dominating religion of the country, Roman Catholicism, enjoyed privileges and freedoms not granted to evangelicals. During the 1930s, authorities in the smaller towns demanded that Ralph Williams and his assistants obtain written permission to enter a town and hold services. This supposedly granted them freedom, but usually disturbances erupted, which resulted in protesters throwing objects at the visiting missionaries who were many times arrested and jailed overnight.

Factions opposing the Roman Catholic Church were considered Communists. Because of this, Ralph Williams' life was threatened on several occasions. Once, he was even put in a lineup to be shot, but a friend happened on the scene and delivered him. Years later, Paul would be accused of being a Communist and ordered from the country.

This was life in El Salvador when we arrived. Instead of elections, the government changed hands through violent revolutions. The open persecution of Christians occurred usually in the smaller towns. The Catholic Church was the center or focal point of every town or village.

A gathering of Christians was meeting in a home directly across the street from the town square in the village of La Palma. Paul was the speaker. This infuriated a large noisy crowd of people congregating in the square. Without warning, men began throwing large skyrockets toward the open door of the home where Paul was speaking. The worshippers closed the door and wooden window shutters just seconds before a skyrocket exploded at the door entrance, forcing the believers to remain secluded in the hot stuffy room.

After several people responded to the call to accept Christ as their Savior and the service ended, the congregation continued to sing and give thanks to God in the stifling room until 2 a.m., when the rowdies disbanded.

On another occasion at a procession, antagonists incited by a local priest threw stones over a six-foot hedge into a Saturday afternoon service Paul was conducting on the patio of a spacious home. Other demonstrators tossed paper bags full of poison ivy leaves, which broke open as they fell, causing burns to many people, particularly to a little girl. A few local citizens stooped low enough to fling cans with urine over the hedge onto the people of the evangelical gathering.

On Good Friday in every city and town of El Salvador large processions carry an image of Christ in a glass casket through the streets for "The Holy Burial"—burying the effigy of Jesus in a church until the next year. One year we happened to arrive in El Salvador from the United States on Good Friday. The people screamed at us for driving over the dead body of Christ and threw stones and garbage at us.

On another Good Friday in a little town, Paul spotted a few blocks ahead one of these large processions, so he parked his car on a side street to wait for its passing. A very large woman recognized Paul as an evangelical minister. She strode up to the car, and with a clenched hand Wham! She almost gave him a mouthful of teeth. Without uttering a word she stared at Paul, her expression filled with angry contempt. Then the woman rejoined the long procession and never looked back.

A young neighbor girl, curious about why we wanted to live in her country, came often to visit us in our home. In his expla-

3

nation one day, Paul quoted a Scripture from the Bible. Immediately she protested, covering her ears, saying she wasn't permitted to read or hear quotes from the Bible. Some people who had received religious tracts hid them from their families because the tracts were denounced as subversive material and were considered the work of the devil.

Because of a revolt against the government in El Salvador, we went to Guatemala for the birth of a robust second son, Gene Otto, on February 5, 1945. When we returned we moved to the capital city, San Salvador. Blessed by his Latin culture and knowledge of Spanish, Paul ministered in churches and taught in the four-month sessions of the Men's Bible School twice a year. He spent almost every weekend sleeping in hammocks, eating meager fare, and returning home rejoicing over possibly a dozen new converts.

At the same time, his heart grieved because of reaching so few people for Christ. His anxiety increased when he read an article in The Pentecostal Evangel, a Christian magazine, which stated that the heathen world was growing one-third faster than the Christian world was growing.

"At that rate," Paul lamented, "we Christians are fighting a losing battle. People are going to hell faster than we can reach them with the message of Christ."

Paul pondered constantly on how to reach the masses. His heart cried, "There has to be a way to reach these sad-faced people who are steeped in religious rituals, unaware that the God of love wants to live in their hearts."

His analysis indicated that the Christian church was failing to fulfill God's plan! Then suddenly realizing that he was the church, Paul felt responsible. In anguish he cried, "God, what can I do? What do You want me to do?"

Paul's constant thought, ambition, and life focused on reaching the masses with the love of Christ.

Chapter 1
A Light in the Darkness

The people living in darkness have seen a great light
(Matthew 4:16).

"Radio!" Paul's excitement and volume grew each time he repeated the word. "Why can't I use radio to preach the gospel of Jesus Christ? No one else is using this medium in Latin America, so why can't I tell the Salvadoran people about Jesus through radio?"

Days became weeks, then months as Paul paced the floor, his head bowed, ignorant of family activities as he meditated on the radio concept and speculated on how he could obtain radio time when he had no money or broadcasting equipment. He wrote to friends in the United States, telling them of his idea of using radio as an evangelism tool. Sadly, no one responded to his letters—not even to say no.

He mentioned his evangelism inspiration to a colleague, and this time the response was immediate. "Forget it, Pablo. You don't have a proper voice for radio."

Then in a biannual reunion of Central American missionaries, Paul posed his question in an afternoon session. "What would you think of a missionary dedicating himself full time to radio ministry?" After a lengthy silence that became embarrassing, attendees ignored Paul's subject and moved on to other business.

Ignoring the insulting remark about his voice and the lack of interest of other missionaries, Paul remembered how four concerned friends lowered a sick man through the roof into the presence of Jesus. "Why can't I," half talking to himself and envisioning the possibility, "lower Jesus through the antenna into the presence of the spiritually ill?"

Determined to utilize radio evangelism, Paul chose YSU, the most prestigious—and the most costly—radio station in San Salvador.

"The influence of a prime radio station," Paul told me, "would qualify the message and is worth the extra expense, because the gospel of Christ is the most valuable message in the world."

Paul went to radio station YSU and studied the programming from all angles until he understood every detail. Without equipment or funds, Paul signed a contract for a daily 15-minute radio program to broadcast on their three network stations that blanketed all of El Salvador. The undertaking would cost $133 a month.

YSU accepted Paul's radio contract with the promise that within three months he would obtain a professional recorder, even though he had no idea how or where he'd get professional equipment. The only time slot YSU had available was 4:30 p.m., the worst listening hour of the day, but Paul grabbed it because it was an "open door" for ministry.

With great excitement, Paul recorded his first gospel radio program for July 1, 1955.

The garage of our house did not contain a car; rather, it was a storeroom for Bibles. Then it became Paul's recording studio. Stifling heat because there was no air conditioning and outside noises and barking dogs made it impossible to record programs during the day. With a borrowed tape recorder propped on a metal missionary barrel, late in the quiet of night, he recorded his radio programs.

As Paul was recording his first program, he knew listeners couldn't spell Finkenbinder, so he told them to write to Hermano Pablo (Brother Paul). He never imagined that one day his radio name would become a household name in the Hispanic world.

Two weeks later, Rev. Roy Stewart of Dallas, Texas, while speaking at a ministers' conference in El Salvador, visited Paul as he recorded a program. "How are you paying for the airtime, Paul?"

"Frankly, Roy, I'm not."

Momentarily speechless, Roy stared at Paul. "Then how can you be on the air?"

Paul flashed a big grin at his friend. "I guess because I have until the end of the month to make my first payment."

Roy sat at our typewriter and wrote a lengthy letter to a minister friend, H. C. Noah, in Dallas, telling him of the need for finances for a new radio project. Paul was delighted with the letter, but then he remembered the letters he had written that had received no responses, not even a "no".

Roy Stewart left the next day. Paul's mood alternated between gloom and euphoria. One thought repeatedly ran through his head: How can Rev. Noah respond to the need of someone who signed an unfunded radio contract?

However, on July 30, 1955, a letter arrived from H. C. Noah. In it was a check for $140 ($133 for the monthly broadcast fee and $7 extra for tape expenses) and the unbelievable promise of monthly support. Rev. Noah honored this marvelous monthly pledge for the 17 years he was pastor of the Oak Cliff Assembly of God Church of Dallas.

Another great miracle occurred when the young people of the Speed the Light program in Colorado provided funds for the professional recorder Paul assured the radio station manager that he would obtain within 90 days.

Ever the visionary of ways to expand the outreach of the gospel of Jesus, Paul dreamed of owning two tape recorders so that he could make copies of his radio program for another station.

We received a letter from Rev. Ben La Fon, a missionary in Santa Rosa de Copan, Honduras, saying he could hear our program faintly and wondered if it would be possible for Paul to make copies of the programs for a local Honduran radio station. The Rev. Gordon Lindsay of the Christ for the Nations Ministry in Dallas was in our home that week. He exclaimed, "This is terrific, Paul! I'll pay the $26.00 a month for the station in Honduras."

In three months' time, Paul became an international radio broadcaster!

Requests for the program in other countries challenged Paul's faith as he continued sharing the greatest story ever told, as well as being responsible for their station time. Rev. Lindsay continued sending financial support and in reality birthed the international ministry of Hermano Pablo.

Although Paul's target audience was the nonbeliever, he naively and unwisely called his radio program The Evangelical Voice of the Assemblies of God, expecting to reach people with the gospel message.

Correspondence revealed he was reaching only three percent of his desired audience. Years later he changed the name of the broadcast to "The Church of the Air" (La Iglesia Del Aire). He discontinued using hymns and instead started using musical orchestrations, which increased the correspondence from unbelievers to 10 then 12 percent. Within the next five years, many stations in Central and South America were carrying the broadcast.

In December 1955, six months after Paul started his radio programs, YSU made an independent survey of its listening audience. Administrators of the radio station were astonished to learn that Hermano Pablo's afternoon radio program at the poor hour of 4:30 in the afternoon was second only to a 6 p.m. newscast.

One evening in a guarded, hushed tone—as though fearful of his own desires—Paul voiced to me his secret ambition of his radio ministry: "My prayer is that my daily Spanish radio program will be aired on 100 radio stations, and that my voice will always make people think of God."

Paul and I held hands and prayed together that God would use Paul's voice as His representative in the Hispanic world and make the 100-station daydream a reality.

Chapter 2
The Power of That Gospel Light

At the name of Jesus, the demons left the room screaming
(Matthew 8:29, paraphrased).

A wretched-looking man appeared at our door. "I'm looking for Hermano Pablo, the person who has a radio program." Paul invited the obviously distraught man into his office and listened to an unbelievable tale.

"My name is Antonio. Ever since I can remember, demons have harassed my life. They continuously have me under their influence. Demons control my mind; their voices constantly compel me to do wicked deeds, which have destroyed my marriage. These malevolent spirits keep me from working and make me an evil, menacing influence in my community. My own mother has put me out of her home several times because I make life intolerable for her.

"I don't just recognize the horrific demons by the shocking sounds they create; I've witnessed them," the man said. "When I first glimpsed these unbelievably gruesome living things, I wanted to die. These terrifying creatures, 12- to 18-inches high, have large ears, hideous eyes, and a fiendish grin. They are constant reminders that I am subservient to them and can never get away.

"In the night, the demons put hot irons on my feet and prick my body with hot needles. My family has seen the pricks and burns on my body when I wake up in the morning. All of my life has been horrible and miserable, Hermano Pablo. I've tried several times to end my life.

"Three months ago, I happened to listen to your 'The Church of the Air' radio program. For the first time in my miserable life, I felt a glimmer of hope. Oh, how those fiendish demons danced around, screaming, fighting me, and demanding I turn off your program when it came on the air at 4:30 in the afternoon! When you talked about Jesus' love and power, your words gave me the ability to resist the demons and continue listening to your program.

"Last week you talked about demons, their reality, and their power to harm, but you also spoke about Christ, His love for humans and His divine power over demons. That day, like never before, I fought a continuous temptation to turn off your radio program at the persistence of the angry demons screaming at me.

"After your words about Jesus having more power than demons, in your closing prayer you demanded that demons depart in Jesus' name. The noisy demons, flying near the ceiling, fled screaming from the room at the mention of Jesus' name, and I was alone with peaceful quietness I never knew existed. I feel like God is inside me.

"I've been searching for you all week, for your explanation regarding what happened and what to do now. I feel freedom from the demanding power of those wicked demons, although I can still hear them calling out to me from a distance. I'm afraid they'll come closer to me."

With a knot in his throat, Paul sat spellbound at Antonio's detailed description of horrible demon possession. He explained God's plan of salvation to Antonio and asked if he would like to

14

invite Jesus into his heart. Antonio readily agreed and prayed with Paul, inviting Jesus to be the Lord of his life.

Antonio's countenance changed instantly from a hopeless appearance to one of tranquil peace—the outward manifestation of an inner change of heart.

Paul prayed again for Antonio. He handed Antonio a Bible, indicating where to read, and directed him to a church near his home. This new brother in Christ departed, composed and wearing a radiant smile.

A year later Paul saw a vibrant Antonio in a church, happy, and full of energy. He was holding down a job, and his marriage had been happily restored.

Antonio praised God for complete deliverance from the power of demons.

"Can Jesus help us?" was the anguished question of two elderly women.

"We're looking for Hermano Pablo. Can you tell us where he lives?" an older woman and her daughter asked in unison.

The day was Thursday and Paul was scheduled to preach in a church on the other side of San Salvador. He was running to the car when these two women met him at the door. He stopped, giving the mother and daughter his complete attention. "I am Hermano Pablo."

Demonstrating great anguish, they took turns telling their story, one picking up where the other left off.

"We have walked four miles from Colonia La Rabida, searching for you as our last hope. In your radio program, we heard you clearly say that Jesus can meet every need. We have an enormous need. Our 12-year-old daughter (granddaughter to the older woman) must go into an orphanage because we are incapable of earning enough from our tortilla sales to feed her. Can your Jesus help us?"

No longer anxious regarding the church service, Paul prayed for the grief-stricken mother and grandmother, whose tears stained their worried faces. He quoted Scriptures and assured them that Jesus loved them and would answer their prayers. He wrote down the name of the pastor and the church in their area, explaining that the pastor would give them more details about the Jesus who promises to help them.

Two weeks later, that pastor thanked Paul profusely for the free tortillas he was receiving, adding that an elderly mother and her daughter had accepted Christ on a Friday night. The next day their miracle began.

The women made their livelihood by making tortillas and selling them at their doorstep. At noon on this day they ran out of tortilla dough and had to run quickly to buy more supplies. The same "tortilla miracle" happened at night, the next day, and the next. People stood in line at their door for tortillas, neglecting their former stands where they typically bought their tortillas.

The women, who had given their lives to Jesus, rejoiced because they sold enough tortillas so that their 12-year-old child didn't have to live in an orphanage. This happened because Jesus meets every need! Jesus heard the desperate cry of these women and He met their need.

Chapter 3
More Gospel Light

Evangelical crusades, with emphasis on divine healings,
changed the spiritual atmosphere of El Salvador.

In 1954 and 1955, Paul, David Stewart, and Arthur Lindvall invited Evangelist Richard Jeffery and his wife, Elva, to El Salvador to hold evangelistic crusades. On their first visit, the Jefferys ministered in San Miguel in the far eastern part of El Salvador, where hundreds of people accepted Christ as their Savior. Not only did they receive their salvation, but the new converts also received physical healing.

One of many converts in San Miguel was Carlos Castro, a crop duster, who used pesticides to fumigate crops. Carlos, an ex-army man, was a typical Latin American: a womanizer, a heavy drinker, and disloyal in his dealings. He arrogantly carried and displayed in his billfold pictures of himself with his women friends, to the torment of his wife, Graciela. The walls of his home, ornamented with bullet holes he created when he returned home drunk, were proof of his belligerent, demanding lifestyle.

Graciela accepted Christ as her Lord and Savior when she observed the drastic, 180-degree change in Carlos's life. However, she continued with her provocative lifestyle of wearing scandalous clothing, which she wore even to church services.

Carlos prohibited anyone speaking to her regarding her dress style, and in a short time, she changed. It was a lesson to believers that God's Holy Spirit would do the necessary work in her life.

In 1955, Richard and Elva Jeffery and son, Gene, returned the second time to El Salvador for services in San Salvador, the country's capital. They planned to rent a house and hire a live-in helper; however, Elva fell and broke her leg during the car trip to Salvador, making it impossible for them to manage a home. Consequently, we invited the three Jefferys into our home with our five children during the three months they were in San Salvador.

Our house was unique. The bathroom occupied the nicest corner of the square house. With three bedrooms set in a row, it was necessary to pass through the middle bedroom to use the facility. Heavy curtains over the lattice doorways demanded respect by everyone in the three bedrooms. Our three daughters occupied the middle transitory room; our sons, Paul and Gene, and Gene Jeffery slept in the garage; and the adult couples occupied the end bedrooms.

Every day was extremely busy and challenging for everyone. One very warm day, our 13-year-old son, Gene, came home from school covered with a measles rash. This taxed my physical as well as my spiritual endurance. I took one look at Gene's condition and calmly, boldly, and confidently claimed God's promise in Psalm 91:10 that no plague would come nigh our dwelling. Every indication of measles disappeared from our son's body! He returned to school the next day, and God protected the rest of the family from the plague of measles.

I had the daily task of preparing meals for a half-dozen crusade leaders besides our family and the Jefferys. Every afternoon and evening, in a large open lot beside our home, Richard played his accordion, Paul his saxophone, and missionary Stewart led joyful singing before the preaching of God's Word.

Paul translated Jeffery's messages, which became my Spanish lessons as I listened first to English and then to the Spanish translation.

Hundreds of people received divine healing through Jeffery's prayer of faith in God, and the miraculous testimonies of healings that were heard daily from the platform. It was exciting to observe once-deaf people turn their heads when they heard an airplane overhead, to see goiters disappear, to witness blinded eyes now seeing, to watch backs and lame limbs healed-all in response to prayer.

One extraordinary healing was that of a man who had been deaf from birth. He had no outer ears, no orifices where his ears should have been. But after his healing, he heard perfectly from both sides of his head. Our daughter Bonnie taught this man to speak many words. Remarkably, he and all healed deaf mutes could repeat words in English with no trace of Spanish accent and could speak Spanish as any other Hispanic.

Religious, non-evangelical leaders in San Salvador were not happy with the evangelistic crusade. Daily the newspapers carried criticisms against the singing and the reported healings. Ultimately, Richard Jeffery was ordered to appear in court for healing people without a proper medical license.

Evangelist Jeffery stood before the stern-faced judge, who had the power to send him to prison for 13 years, when Julia Lopez, a neighbor of the judge, walked into the courtroom unannounced. The judge stared at his once severely crippled neighbor in utter bewilderment; he was astonished that she no longer walked on crutches. He demanded an explanation.

"This man," she said pointing to Richard Jeffery, "prayed to God for my healing, and God delivered me of my bondage."

"Did Evangelist Jeffery touch you?" the inflexible judge inquired of this only witness.

"No, the evangelist made one prayer for everyone without touching anyone. By the power of God I am healed," Julia declared jubilantly.

The judge, with no contrary witnesses, had no other recourse but to throw out the case and free Jeffery. The charge of healing without a license was dismissed.

Weeks before the crusade ended, someone bought the lot next to our house to stop the afternoon and evening services. But another man offered a better lot, so the services continued without a day of interruption.

When the Jefferys returned to the States, a caravan of 11 large city buses plus numerous carloads of people accompanied the Jefferys to the Guatemalan border in an expression of love. It was a spectacular whole-day event, yet the critical anti-evangelical newspaper journalists and radio newscasters did not report one word of this abnormally large evangelical event.

Satan tried to stop the crusade first by breaking Elva's leg, and then by false accusations, followed by forcing the services to transfer to another location. But God continued to edify His church with healings and miracles.

Thanks to Richard Jeffery's three-month crusade and to missionary Arthur Lindvall's dedicated efforts to harvest the results of the many conversions, twelve new churches were established. Lindvall weekly met with a dozen young dedicated future pastors from among our believers—training, instructing, and guiding them in teaching new believers about their faith in Jesus Christ.

Two years later the large Evangelistic Center under construction in San Salvador was the hub for these new churches. These new works were increasing in size, but the leaders had great difficulty in finding adequate places to baptize the believers, so they requested the use of the baptistery of the Evangelistic Center.

Half of the people thought using the baptistery before the center was completed would deter the completion of the building. The other half saw no reason not to use the baptistery as is. The problem fermented for months, and even the superintendent of the Assemblies of God could not bring the two factions to an agreement. Then they invited Paul to speak one Saturday to a gathering of both groups in the Evangelistic Center.

Walking with Paul the three blocks from our home to the center that afternoon, I asked him what he intended to say. He looked at me and shrugged his shoulders. "Hon, I haven't the slightest idea of what to say, but I know God will illuminate me when I get up to speak."

The Evangelistic Center seated 3,000 people. That day it was filled to capacity, evenly divided between the two factions. All attendees looked expectantly to Paul as he stood before them. After greeting the group, he spoke about five minutes against using the baptistery before the construction was finalized. Of course, he won the approval of half of the group.

Then he spoke about using the baptistery as is. Then he finalized his thoughts with a question. "What explanation would I give to God for not using the baptistery when there is no other place available?"

Instantly, the problem resolved itself with everyone shouting a hearty "Amen!"

God used Paul not only to bring the gospel of Christ to the unsaved but also to minister among the brethren.

However, Paul had not always been at peace with himself or with God.

Chapter 4
God Called a Rebellious Youth

Zion Bible Institute took a rebellious, obstinate, ambitious youth named Paul and fashioned a useful man of God for His purposes!

Despondent, the impatient youth crossed out the "yes" he had hastily written with the blue permanent ink fountain pen and wrote "no" above it. "Surely the person who accepts my untidy questionnaire will understand the turmoil in my heart and mind when he or she sees I've changed my answer," the youth reasoned.

He was an adolescent, just barely 17. This was most certainly the first major decision he was making on his own. Frantically, he attempted to erase the unattractive ink smudge on the document before him. The blemish only worsened. The youth slumped in his seat in the Greyhound Bus that was taking him away from home to a new beginning—to a world without parental supervision.

In his mind was the question, Are you presently seeking the Holy Spirit experience? His "yes" answer was an absolute falsehood. He not only wanted to alter his dishonest response, he also longed to conceal his obvious lack of spiritual interest.

Actually, the ambitious youth was impatient to get away from God and religious principles. He loved his family, but he disliked submitting to family and church regulations. He somehow convinced his unyielding father that he should get away from the ungodly high school influence. His father shrewdly directed his rebellious son to the influence of a spiritual institution, unenthusiastically agreeing: "Okay, I'll let you put off the last year of high school if you will attend a Christian school of my choosing."

Attending any place that was religious did not appeal to this young man, but his resolute father offered him no alternative. "My entire life I've heard and lived by biblical standards, and the thought of studying the Bible further is not part of my youthful ambition."

Two years earlier, he and his friend Gilberto endeavored to run away from their homes and parental authority. With money stolen from his blind brother's piggy bank, he put a few clothes into a paper bag and hid it in the trunk of his father's car, intending to slip out of church with his friend and hitchhike to California. As planned, he and Gilberto sneaked out of the church. They tried to steal rides on the back of trolley cars, but the sharp-eyed conductors frightened away the runaways. By midnight, they had made it only as far as the Brooklyn Bridge.

Both boys had forgotten that nights are cold, and had carelessly neglected to bring warm jackets. Adding to their predicament, no drivers offered to pick up the young hitchhikers in the middle of the night. Their only solution was to return home and accept parental punishment.

The frightened runaway youth was astonished that, although his parents had called the police, they said absolutely nothing of his foolish escapade. Instead, his father took him to his church the next morning, where one of his assistants talked to the youth nearing manhood at length regarding the consequences of sowing and reaping.

Weeks later the young man's father kindly explained his action. "Son, next time you want to run away, tell us and we'll buy you some luggage, give you money, and we can write to each other."

What a father! He understood that he had completed his parental training and from now on, his impulsive son would learn to live by his own decisions.

Recollections of home life with his two sisters and two blind brothers—and contemplations of what the future might hold—occupied his mind as he neared his destination. The miles ended and the would-be adult found himself trembling before the president of Zion Bible Institute, Mrs. Christine Gibson. She briefly studied the entrance document, making no comment regarding the ink blemish. Then she turned her gaze to him and scrutinized him with her sensitive steel blue eyes. "Well, young man, you are here. Welcome to Zion!"

Zion's newest arrival, whose name was Paul, was not entirely elated with his preliminary impressions of the school his father had chosen. As at home, there were regulations to follow and principles to uphold. Obedient by nature, Paul settled in with his roommate, Johnny Sindorf, attended classes, and endeavored to absorb the scholastic material. He was not accustomed to applying his intellect to education, but here at least he didn't have to respond to his parents.

However, the youth had not anticipated that the internal restlessness that threatened to overwhelm him would continue and leave him feeling completely worthless. Initially he thought he missed his family, but he soon realized he was feeling the same emptiness he had felt whenever he bowed his head in prayer at home or in his father's church.

Paul entered Zion as rebellious as Jonah had been when God called him to preach in Nineveh. He was not interested in following his father's footsteps in ministry—especially as a missionary, because of the many hardships his family had experienced as missionaries earlier in his life. That type of existence was of no interest to him, because his two brothers were born blind and two other siblings lay buried in Puerto Rico, his birthplace. Because of the delicate physical condition of his mother, his family returned to the United States to reside when he was 15. In addition, he associated the mission field with poverty—unending poverty!

Paul recalled an incident that his mother recounted to him many times. He wondered about the meaning. When he was only six months of age, his mother was sitting in her bedroom, caressing and adoring her firstborn son. She unmistakably heard a distinct voice. He's not yours; he's Mine.

Terrified, she clutched her baby closer to her breast, turning to locate the voice's source. She believed it meant he was going to die, so she exclaimed, "No, don't take him; he's mine."

Clearly, she heard the voice again. He's not yours; and he's Mine.

She eventually understood God's call on Paul's life and carried in her heart the consciousness that God had claimed her Pablito for His purposes. Those special purposes that God evidently had planned for him were queries still unanswered and unimportant to Paul as he attended Zion.

Paul couldn't help feeling disappointment, because his classmates demonstrated a deep-seated contentment and happiness that had eluded him. Fellow students prayed, rejoiced, sang, and some even danced in the Spirit, indicative of a contentment that he was not able to grasp or comprehend.

Paul enjoyed admiring all the pretty girl students at Zion; however, he was permitted to appreciate the female students only from a distance because Zion frowned upon boy-girl friendships. But even the attention-grabbing girls couldn't diminish the heaviness in his heart, especially when night came and sleep evaded him.

The weeks became months, and Paul realized the uneasiness always came to him when he closed his eyes to rest or in chapel services when the students prayed or sang enthusiastically.

One evening during an evening chapel service while hunched in his seat with his face buried in his hands, Paul's mind churned in turmoil. He ignored the devotional singing of his classmates. In a desperate cry, he called out to God. "God, I can't handle this nothing-to-live-for, empty sensation! I surrender my life to You for anything You desire of me."

In a flash, looming before his eyes stood a vast field of ripe cotton, and before the harvesters could pick them, the white cotton balls were falling to the ground and rotting. Instantly, Paul sensed that the cotton balls represented souls dying without the knowledge of Christ, and that God expected him to tell them of His salvation.

The scene changed and he observed the vast expanse of cotton in a lapse dissolve into the cinnamon-colored faces of the Hispanic people with whom he grew up in Puerto Rico. There were millions of expectant expressions and close-up scenes revealing people holding up their arms and imploring, "You have something to tell us; don't abandon us."

When those visions ended, in his mind's eye he saw his head on the base of a guillotine with the blade hanging menacingly over him, ready to sever his head. Completely exhausted and resigned to God's desire, he submissively responded, "Lord, if you won't have it any other way, go ahead and pull the latchstring. Kill me, I'll go."

The instant his disobedient heart surrendered, Paul realized there was no latchstring, no guillotine, or chopping block. And the purposelessness in his aching heart was gone. He felt like he had been an incarcerated bird released from the restrictions of a confining cage, granting him complete freedom. The obstinacy and the unruly spirit that he himself could not comprehend and had confused him for too long no longer existed.

The next day he relayed his vision to his roommate, who dabbled in photography. Paul asked him to put his picture in a certain area of a South American map. When they compared the map with the outline of South America, his picture and the scene of his vision was directly over Bolivia.

Although Paul was only a youthful 17-year-old student, his life took on new meaning, expectancy, and rejoicing because God wanted him to be His messenger to Bolivia.

The once restless, impatient youth realized that the restlessness and meaninglessness in his heart was rebellion against God, the only One who could fill that vacancy and give him peace.

Paul, the once-rebellious youth, returned a second year to Zion.

Eagerly and enthusiastically, Paul immersed himself into his studies, augmenting his knowledge of God's Word. The Rev. Christine Gibson, founder and president of Zion, was an exceptional woman of compassion and faith. She had absolute, unconditional faith in God to meet His people's every need. She never purchased anything without having the funds on hand to pay for it.

On numerous occasions when the school was without finances and there was no food for the next meal, God answered prayer and supplied the need miraculously. Usually an accident occurred in the city, with a truckload of food, fish, or breads strewn in the street. Zion could have the food if the students would pick it up.

One exceptionally cold December morning, the rooms throughout the entire Zion school complex were ice-cold, with the bathroom water like liquid ice. The kitchen stoves bordering one side of the dining room were gas and radiated a bit of heat into the dining room, which was the warmest room of Zion's buildings. Everyone ate breakfast while wrapped in his or her winter coats.

Sister Gibson requested that the students return to the slightly warmed dining room after breakfast for a special message—always an hour-long about God's obligation to answer our prayers.

"God promises to meet our needs," she explained. "But if we can answer our own prayers, God is not obligated."

Sister Gibson concluded her timely message regarding our and God's obligations, leaving the student body with a strong sense of responsibility. Paul and every other student rushed at once to their rooms to bring whatever monies they possessed for the much-needed coal to heat Zion's buildings. The largest contribution was $80 from a student who was saving for a suit. Paul contributed his dollar and nickels to the mound of bills and coins piled on a large open Bible.

The moment the last coin was offered on the Bible, a member of Zion's Worship Center from the state of Maine—more than a hundred miles away—knocked at the door. He entered and requested permission to speak. The account of his humble obedience to the prompting of God's Holy Spirit affected everyone keenly.

"God awakened me at three o'clock this cold morning from a sound sleep, informing me that your buildings are cold because you have no fuel or money to buy fuel. I fought the temptation to remain in my warm bed, because the temperature was colder there than here, but in obedience to the Holy Spirit's nudging, I loaded my truck with coal and rushed here as fast as I could. Sister Gibson, if your fine students will assist me in unloading the coal, we'll get some warmth into all your buildings." He concluded by motioning toward his truck outside.

Gasps broke the solemn silence; then applause occurred, followed by exhilaration because that timely coal delivery was an unbelievable material-and-spiritual confirmation of God's promise. God supplied fuel to heat Zion's buildings after students obediently contributed what they could of their own means before expecting God to answer their supplication for fuel.

The school president's special message about God's accountability was a powerful teaching that Paul observed and profited from all his life. And these faith experiences made a great impact on him.

Longing for a deeper presence of the Lord in his life, Paul returned to the tabernacle one night after the evening service and threw himself on the floor, asking God for the infilling of the Holy Spirit baptism with the evidence of speaking in another tongue.

All of his family, as well as the church of which his father was pastor, followed the Pentecostal doctrine that is described in the book of Acts in the Bible. That experience gave students the fearlessness and boldness to testify to the Lord's power and faithfulness and to dedicate their lives to the Lord. Paul felt God's call on his life, but he sensed his lack of the Holy Spirit's anointing.

He sought the Lord in prayer, crying out to Him for the Holy Spirit's evidence of speaking in tongues. He sensed Christ lovingly admonish him. "You shouldn't be praying to speak in another language; you need to ask for more of Jesus in your life."

In his anxiety to receive God's blessing on his life, he was asking for the "evidence" of Holy Spirit instead of the Giver of the Holy Spirit. A few hours later, when he opened his eyes after receiving the desired anointing—and speaking in an unknown tongue—he saw several students and his favorite professor, Leonard Heroo, praying around him.

Gone were his timidity and indecision. Now his life radiated the peace and confidence that all of us see in Paul today. He says, "The baptism of the Holy Spirit has given me the strength, confidence, and faith that is the power of my life."

God honored Sister Gibson's implicit faith in His Word. She effectively instilled faith in numberless students, including an impressionable 18-year-old youth.

Chapter 5
Captivated

Paul and I met and fell in love during Paul's third and last year at Zion Bible Institute.

Paul arrived late at Zion his third year, after spending the summer with his parents in Cuba.

In Paul's words: "Sunday night after the Thanksgiving weekend, I was at the foot of the stairs that led down to Zion's dining room when suddenly a feminine angel with dark hair appeared on the top step of the stairs. As my eyes caught sight of her, my heart began pounding, then seeming to stop and beat alternately, leaving me breathless.

"The next morning, I entered the dining room from a backdoor and saw the same charming angel again, who happened to be glancing my way. When our eyes met for a fleeting second, I was totally captivated; my heart beat wildly in my chest, leaving me feeling weak and faint and at the same time elated."

I, Linda, recall that it was the Wednesday before Thanksgiving that I answered a knock at the door of the women's dorm at Zion. When I opened the door, there stood a handsome student inquiring about Maxine. I climbed the stairs to inform Maxine that the car and driver taking her home for the holiday weekend had arrived. I hunted for her, but Maxine wasn't in. When I returned to the door to inform the attractive young scholar, I was suddenly struck with jealousy because he had asked for Maxine. I didn't even know who he was.

Sunday evening I saw the same fellow at the foot of the stairs, standing up straight with his hands behind his back, observing me. I felt tingly all over, but I didn't permit myself to make eye contact with him.

The next morning while quietly seated at the breakfast table with seven other classmates, I was startled by the sound of rapid footsteps entering the backdoor. And, lo, there was that same young man again. Our eyes met from across the room for a split second, leaving me with an unusual and strange sensation. Looking back at my friends around the table, everyone was staring at my obviously flushed face. My table hostess reproachfully demanded, "Who is he? What is his name? Why is he looking at you?"

All I could do to answer each rapid-fire question was to shrug my shoulders and say, "I don't know! I don't know!"

The youth must have inquired of someone and learned that my name was Linda. Then he waited patiently at the top of the staircase for me while I completed my kitchen duty. When I came near the exit of the building, he very graciously acknowledged me with my first lesson in a foreign language. "Do you know what your name means in Spanish?"

I shook my head, indicating that I had no idea.

"Linda means 'beautiful'." His undeniable tone of admiration flustered me so that I couldn't think of anything to say. I grabbed my coat and rushed out the door.

Bobby Washington, one of Paul's friends, claimed to have observed Cupid shooting his arrow when our eyes met in the dining room. He offered to pass me Paul's note, asking for my picture.

That evening, against Zion's strict rules, Paul entered the kitchen. He spoke into the air behind me as I rinsed dishes, introducing himself to the girl who had captivated his heart. "My name is Paul Finkenbinder, the son of missionary parents to Puerto Rico, and I'm planning to be a missionary."

This would-be missionary entered the kitchen the next evening and declared aloud so that the entire kitchen crew could hear, "I'm not interested in just having a girlfriend; I want a sweetheart who wants to be a missionary."

I was enchanted with his candid sincerity. This determined-to-have-my-attention fellow, and his plan to be a missionary, really interested me. I, too, had a calling on my life.

At the age of nine, I suffered a severe bout of smallpox that Michigan doctors diagnosed had come from Africa. I had only three spots of the dreaded disease on my body and evidently, this was the cause of my extremely high fever.

One afternoon when my fever was elevated, I had an out-of-body experience or a vision of walking through a long tunnel hand in hand with a tall figure dressed in white. As we passed a dark area on our left, screams of agony and terror filled the air. Instinctively I sensed this was hell, and I clutched the figure's hand tighter. We continued walking, and at the end of the tunnel, we came into bright sunlight, blue skies, chirping birds, and flowers and butterflies in beautiful color hues. I knew this was heaven. I turned to share the marvelous peaceful serenity with the figure in white, but this angel—or was it Christ?—had vanished.

I awakened crying and telling my mother I wanted to die, because I was not feverish in that beautiful place. She listened thoughtfully for a moment before responding tenderly. "Linda, we're fortunate because we know who Jesus is. That place undoubtedly was heaven, but perhaps God wants you to get well so that you can tell people about Jesus' love, because millions of people have never heard His name."

From that moment, I wanted to get well so I could be a missionary and tell people about Jesus.

In my opinion, being a missionary is the highest of vocations, so when Paul said he was going to be a missionary, I was immediately attracted to him. When I entered Zion, I had determined that I would not have a boyfriend unless I received a definite sign. Naturally desiring to be married, yet at the same time frightened to marry the wrong person, I arose early every morning and prayed in a cold attic for God's guidance. Paul was the first male figure who did not incite within me a feeling of fear, but I had to be sure that God approved him for me.

Months later, Paul confided that two weeks after we had met, he wrote his parents telling them he had found the girl he was going to marry.

Dating at Zion was not allowed, but two instructors, Rev. Ed and Sylvia Hill, arranged an outing for us. One day in April 1941, they invited Paul to accompany them on a visit to Henry Garlock, a veteran missionary. They invited me for the same occasion. We each obtained permission from our respective housemothers, guardedly omitting the information that a person of the opposite sex would be in the same car, which was strictly forbidden.

While in the Garlock's home, Ed and Sylvia Hill, along with Henry and his wife, enjoyed watching us fidget as they spoke of another couple who had come to their home in the identical sneaky manner we had.

On our return to Zion, the Hills stopped at a Howard Johnson restaurant for refreshments and suggested Paul and I could eat our ice cream cones in the car. It was a delightful experience for us to be seated together for the very first time—eating, conversing, holding hands, and enjoying our closeness.

In our conversation, Paul expressed that he had loved me from the moment he saw me on the stairs and couldn't get me out of his mind. He needed to know if I felt the same about him. I acknowledged that he had absolutely enthralled my heart with an extraordinary sensation as no other person had. Yes, I did feel affection for him.

Without warning and taking me completely by surprise, Paul, visibly filled with emotion, blurted out, "I love you, Linda. Will you marry me?"

I pondered the monumental question a long moment before looking into his eyes and whispering, "Yes."

Paul put his arm around me, drew me close to him, and kissed me tenderly on my lips, sealing our commitment to each other. I'll always remember that starry night of April 23, 1941, in a car outside a Howard Johnson restaurant: our first date, our first kiss, and my promise to marry Paul.

We finished the year at Zion with a double ambition: to serve God as missionaries and to marry after Paul completed his studies.

Paul graduated from Zion Bible Institute in Providence, Rhode Island, in May 1941. Immediately he made plans to attend Central Bible College in Springfield, Missouri, for a post-graduate course in missions. I too made plans to transfer to the same institute to be close to him.

At 19 years of age, Paul had fully determined that his life's ambition, with me beside him, would be serving God as a missionary in Bolivia.

Chapter 6
Until Death Do Us Part

*I followed Paul to Central Bible Institute (CBI)
in Springfield, Missouri, but on the way, I became fearful of
making the disastrous mistake of marrying Paul
if it was not God's will.*

Traveling by train to Central Bible Institute to be near Paul, I experienced fear of making a lifetime error in marrying Paul. A sister had recently divorced her husband, other married friends were living miserably together, and none of those examples was the kind of marriage I wanted. I asked myself, Should I marry Paul? Was it God's will?

My Bible reading that day was about Gideon, who used a fleece to learn God's will. So I decided to use the same method to ascertain God's will regarding my marrying Paul.

If Paul was paid some monies owed him, he intended to give me an engagement ring when we met again at CBI. Of course, the ring was an exciting anticipation. Would Paul have the ring? Frightened because I loved Paul and wanted to marry him, but fearful of making a lifelong error, my "fleece" would be that if Paul did not have the ring, I would not marry him.

I arrived first at CBI and was unpacking my trunk when I heard Paul's light knock on the door. My heart pounded uncontrollably; I was facing the greatest decision of my life. I lifted a swift, silent, and solemn prayer to be faithful to my vow. I opened the door and my heart screamed with joy at seeing my heartthrob expressively radiating his love for me. My heart was still pounding excitely as Paul hugged me affectionately.

"I have something for you," he said.

That was the happiest moment of my life.

That same evening, under the stars, on a small footbridge at CBI, Paul put a tiny blue diamond ring on my finger, sealing our commitment to marry.

Paul learned an unforgettable lesson at CBI. One evening he wanted to join the fellows for some refreshments from the snack bar—a soft drink and a bag of potato chips. However, he had no money, with the exception of a single dime in his dresser drawer, a tithe separated for God from a previous donation. After considerable deliberation, he decided to borrow the solitary dime from God. He later said, "Those were the soggiest potato chips and that drink was the most insipid soft drink I have ever tasted."

Repentance for using what had been separated for God haunted him many days, because he needed soap, toothpaste, and other toiletries, and no money arrived from anyone.

One day while strolling with me though the CBI campus, his conscience unrelentingly annoyed him over the robbed dime. Paul confessed the incident, relating the consequences directly with his current needs. Both of us grew up believing that God meets our needs if we faithfully honor and obey Him, which for us definitely included paying a tithe.

That day I had received $4 from a friend. I good-naturedly suggested that if I separated 50-cents for God, it would be enough to cancel Paul's debt. Pensive, he thanked me. Yet both of us wondered if God would consider Paul's debt paid if I took care of it. Our concern centered on the fact that we were engaged but not married yet.

When Paul and I met for dinner that evening, he was clearly excited. In a rush of words, he reported that his roommate, Paul Wright, who knew nothing of his financial plight, felt directed of God to give him $8. Immediately, Paul associated the payment of his tithe debt with the supply of his needs, realizing that using God's money was a form of thievery. This occurred more than 60 years ago, and Paul has never again failed to pay tithe.

In December 1941 the United States declared war against Japan. This event changed our marriage plans set for May at the end of the school year. At the end of the semester in January 1942, after Paul's completion of classes on missions, we decided to leave CBI, marry, and begin life together, even though we were deeply concerned that Uncle Sam would call Paul to war. However, when the summons came in February, Paul wrote a letter explaining he had spent the last three-and-a-half years preparing for ministry. He was granted a 4-d classification.

Paul's father was in Springfield, Missouri, at that time and agreed to perform the wedding ceremony after a Sunday morning service in the Northside Assembly of God Church. The date was January 25, 1942. Paul and I stood before the congregation, before Dad, and before God, declaring our devotion and fidelity to each other until separated by death. It was a simple ceremony, not the candlelight wedding we had been planning.

We left CBI and traveled by bus to Paul's home in Denver, Colorado. Two weeks later, the superintendant of the Assemblies of God, Jose Ibarra, took us to a small Hispanic mission in Raton,

New Mexico, and surprised Paul with the invitation to give the evening message. The second surprise of the evening was the invitation for us to remain in Raton as pastor of the tiny Hispanic mission of five families.

The war, food rationing, and the constant poverty experiences in Raton challenged the powerful faith lessons we experienced in Zion. The Hispanics were poor, unaccustomed to giving, and many times the offering plate returned with a dime, and occasionally empty.

To supplement our financial insufficiency, we raised rabbits for food and Paul worked part-time in a Safeway store. Dedicated friends in Jamestown, New York, Clarence and Gladys Woodard, literally kept us alive by faithfully sending us $3 or $4 weekly, which made up the greater part of our income.

God never supplied additional provisions until we had eaten the last bit of whatever food we had in the house. One time I purchased a three-pound box of elbow macaroni, which was our only daily fare for several weeks. After we had finished it, I declared I would never buy in quantities again!

One time when Paul's father visited us in Raton, he bought three huge boxes of cornflakes on sale for 27-cents. He intended to take two boxes home with him. But he forgot them. We savored cornflakes with milk (occasionally watered down or with diluted evaporated milk) and sugar. One morning we had a tiny amount of evaporated milk in a small cream pitcher, so watered down it looked blue. Paul poured the entire contents on his cornflakes. When he saw me endeavoring to eat dry cornflakes, which kept escaping from the spoon, he held his cereal bowl over mine, and with his hand, squeezed all he could of the bluish liquid on my cereal. We laughed until we cried at our waterlogged cornflakes and our financial difficulties, but we never believed God had failed us!

We approved the purchase of a large adobe building for a place of worship and made a partition of blankets, later a wall, to form a two-room residence in the back of the building. It usually fell upon us personally to make the $10 monthly payment on the building that had no water, heat, or bathroom facilities. From a spigot on the street Paul brought by the pail full all our supply of water, even for laundry, into our humble abode.

We learned another powerful lesson as we selfishly attempted to compel people to answer our prayers while serving in the mission work in Raton. I was pregnant and we had no food in the house, so one day we decided to visit the five families of the mission. Our hope was that someone would invite us for a meal. One family was eating when we knocked at their door, but they didn't even offer us a corn tortilla.

Discouraged and tired as we trudged toward home with the sizzling sun beating down on us, we complained to God that we had no food in the house, and that it was not fair because we were attempting to fulfill His commission.

As we approached our dwelling in the rear of the adobe church building, we were amazed to see sitting by the back door two very large grocery bags overflowing with groceries. The two godly women pastors of the English Foursquare Church felt led of the Lord to bring us groceries. How embarrassed and penitent we felt before God for attempting to answer our own prayer when we knew He promised to meet our every need and unbeknownst to us already had answered our prayers.

These same two dear women pastors gave me a beautiful baby shower; their efforts provided everything our baby needed (except that our parents already had given us a baby crib and stroller).

Just before our baby, Paul Raymond, arrived on September 4, 1942, Paul took a job as a night taxi driver and rented an apartment across town from our mission. It was great having water and inside facilities, but we were away from the mission.

Paul had too little time for Bible reading and prayer, and we both felt it wasn't what God wanted of us. Because serving God full time was our priority, we gave up the great home conveniences and moved back to the humble old adobe building.

Paul analyzes everything, and one day he solemnly came to me with the suggestion that we pay double tithe instead of the customary 10 percent we had faithfully given to God. Initially I laughed and said, "Twenty percent of nothing isn't harder to give than ten percent."

We seriously discussed the tithe increase and determined to try it. We increased the giving of our scanty income to 20 percent. We were surprised that immediately we began faring better and were able to buy milk for the beautiful son God had given us.

We knew God certainly didn't need the few dollars we gave Him, but our giving demonstrated to God that He is supreme in our lives, and it granted us complete confidence in God's promises for every need.

One day our baby, Paul, had a high fever. It was 1942—war days—and we had no doctor or money for one. Little Paul had had a fever and diarrhea for two or three days. We were frightened because nothing we did to help worked. Paul prayed for our son, "God, you are our Healer, but if You aren't going to heal our baby, we will have to find a doctor." We saw an instantaneous healing. Our baby had absolutely no more diarrhea and his fever left him. He was well!

We were content as we served God in Raton, but being overseas missionaries was our most ardent desire. In May 1943 the Missions Department of the Assemblies of God approved our petition to go to El Salvador as missionaries. We were euphoric!

Chapter 7
Our New Life in El Salvador

With our little son, Paul Raymond, we said good-bye to our families in the United States to begin serving God as missionaries in El Salvador.

We arrived in Santa Ana, El Salvador, November 1943, the evening before Thanksgiving Day, ready to begin the vocation of our dreams.

The first day, special introductory services were held in Templo Betel ("Bethel Temple") church, and, of course, the congregation eagerly gathered to meet the new missionaries. The Harvey Smiths and three other missionary couples, who had traveled with us from the United States, needed introduction and translation, because they did not speak Spanish.

When Paul introduced himself in Spanish, the people were surprised. When he introduced his wife and little son, they gasped in astonishment because he looked so young. We were both 22 years of age. A general complaint among the church leaders was that they had expected a missionary not a boy.

Thanks to Paul's knowledge of Spanish and the Latin culture, he began to minister tirelessly. He traveled all over El Salvador by bus, train, and his mule, Blackie, which young people in Colorado had bought for him. When traveling on his mule, Paul and

Francisco Arbizu, his traveling companion, stopped at night at any ranch along the way. During those trips of five to seven days, Paul returned with numerous flea and bedbug bites, but with only a few converts.

His ever-present longing was to share the message of Christ with the masses, always claiming, "These are my people. I feel more at home with them than I do with North Americans."

We moved from a home across town to be near the church where we were working. We soon called our home "the rat house" because we were definitely the minority. Living conditions were difficult. Many times a partly toothless woman on her way to church provided the only extra food that was given to us except for the typical rice and beans. She would stop by our house and from the basket on her head leave avocados, eggs or fruit, and say the words "May God give you a good day." Tina never knew what her love gifts meant to us.

I became pregnant with our third child and suffered with borderline pernicious anemia. Near the end of my pregnancy, at the suggestion of our superior, Paul requested to return to the United States for my healing and the birth of our child. Our denomination responded with plane fares for the four of us and support for three months in the U.S. Then Paul could decide what he wanted to do.

We were stunned and heartbroken at the turn of events because we realized that if we returned to the United States for my health, we would end our much-cherished missionary career. We loved the Salvadoran people and the ministry, even with the horrible living conditions. Quitting never entered our minds.

We cried, prayed, deliberated, and within a few days, returned the check to the Missions Department. We stated that we were staying in El Salvador and trusting God for my healing, which He faithfully provided.

We returned to the States for furlough on July 3, 1948. We had with us our two sons and daughter, Sharon Ann, born March 6, 1947. During routine physicals, the doctors shocked us when they asked, "Linda, when did you contract tuberculosis?" They assured us it was not active.

We were completely bewildered. We were unaware that I had contracted the disease until we remembered our house was across the narrow street from an albino man who had died of that disease. So somehow I had become infected with it.

During this same check-up, tests revealed no trace of the anemia with which I earlier had been diagnosed. Test marks on my arm remind us even today that our Heavenly Father, sight unseen, was there with us constantly during our most difficult and trying times.

We returned to El Salvador in 1949 for another four-year term of service. Paul continued working with the Christ's Ambassadors young peoples group, which he organized in our first term. He continued his travels to every corner of El Salvador with the priceless message of Jesus Christ.

God blessed us with two more daughters, Joan Adele, born June 5, 1951, and Ellin Ruth, born December 18, 1952. Paul was an outstanding father, giving his children love and companionship. When he returned from his trips, he would get on the floor and romp with the children, playing their little games, strumming his guitar, and singing with them. Neighbors peered through the shutter windows at Paul's playing with the children. They said that they never saw their husbands play with their children like that.

Early in his ministry career Paul learned another important lesson that he has never forgotten. He was invited to be the speaker at the National Conference of the Assemblies of God in El Salvador, which every minister and missionary in the country attended. It was the most important evangelical annual event of the denomination. Being a young and inexperienced conference speaker, Paul was naturally uneasy and fearful as he faced the huge responsibility.

Walking to the church that night, he sensed the Lord saying to him, "Paul, you are worried about speaking tonight because of your fear of not doing well. You are concerned that you won't be a success in front of your friends. Remember that your responsibility is to deliver the message I have put on your heart. If you deliver a great message and receive accolades, you will be blessed; however, if you are a failure in speaking, that will be a fabulous lesson for your ego." It was a lesson he has remembered all his life.

Paul did well with his presentation; his charisma was an asset. But he learned to never again be concerned about his presentations. He prepares, prays, and does his best, and then he forgets it. He delivers God's message and trusts that God will do with the words as He will.

One mission trip, took him on a trip to San Fernando, Honduras. He traveled the first hours by bus to Gramales in northern El Salvador. There he rented a mule for the grueling three-hour trek through the mountains to San Fernando. When he dismounted the mule, he couldn't straighten his body, and walked twisted as though he was still straddling the mule.

After resting in a hammock and eating a typical meal of rice, beans, and fried plantains, he was ready for the evening service, which was in that same one-room home. The people crowded into every available space. While he spoke, his eye caught sight of a Singer sewing machine in one corner of the room. He was curious about how long the sewing machine had been there. His hosts calculated it had been at least 20 years since someone had showed them pictures of sewing machines. They had chosen this model, which came to San Fernando just as he had, on the back of a mule.

Right away, Paul questioned, "How is it that the Singer Sewing Machine Company came to San Fernando 20 years ago and we are just now bringing them the gospel of Jesus Christ?" Of course, he knew the answer. The Singer Company, as well as many other commercial enterprises did not wait for some mystical order before taking their products to the world. These companies knew that the sale of their goods depended on their own marketing efforts.

Paul felt shame and embarrassment that Christians wait for God to tap them on the shoulder before making a move, fearing they might get ahead of God's will. Jesus gave us the command, *"Go into all the world and preach the good news to all creation" (Mark 16:15).*

Paul's heart burned constantly with the desire that the message of Christ would be proclaimed in every home in the Spanish world.

Chapter 8
The Power of Prayer

*Prayer for the believer in God is the greatest power
instrument of life.*

On May 25, 1945, Paul began his homeward journey
from San Miguel, in the eastern part of El Salvador,
with four other ministers of the gospel who had ministered with
him that weekend in a fellowship rally. God blessed the services
tremendously; the men were still rejoicing as they began their
journey toward San Salvador.

The men were traveling in torrential rain in an old 1938
Chevrolet that Paul had inherited from missionary Earl Wilkie,
who had transferred to Bolivia. Driving with bald tires against
the greasy blacktop highway to San Salvador was like sliding on
lubricated glass. Paul knew that any quick maneuver of the steering wheel would be disastrous. Even more dangerous was the
fact that the rapidly swishing windshield wipers were virtually
useless in clearing the view ahead.

Ten miles from San Salvador, rounding a hilly curve to the
right, Paul saw a railroad sign. Literally, five feet farther, train
tracks angled toward him, with a freight train approaching at a
high speed. Paul knew instantly the futility of attempting to cross
the railroad tracks ahead of the fast-moving train racing toward
him.

The only way to avoid a direct front-end collision with the train was to turn the car toward the fifteen-foot drop-off on his left. As he attempted the turn, the greasy asphalt gained control of the old Chevrolet; with a deafening grinding of metal against metal, the car ran into the enormous iron front wheel of the on-coming train.

The completely demolished vehicle gyrated a couple times like a top. The windshield was shattered into a million pieces, except for eighteen inches directly in front of Paul's eyes. Amazingly, the car's engine broke through the firewall under Paul's feet with the steering wheel miraculously bent backward instead of forward which kept it from crushing his body.

Israel Garcia, the front-seat passenger, had leaned down to apply the hand brake, saving his eyes from certain blindness by the shattered glass windshield. A small open wound on Israel's head, his only injury, bled profusely. The three back-seat passengers appeared uninjured. When the train came to a stop a few blocks further down the tracks, authorities registered the time of the accident at 2:13 in the afternoon.

Many passengers on the train ran back to the scene of the accident, looking for a decapitated man. They had seen a headlight rolling down the tracks, mistaking it for a head.

According to Salvadoran law, Paul was guilty of a crime and faced criminal charges if the gash on Israel's head did not heal within eight days. Thanks to God, the injury healed and no criminal charges were filed against Paul.

The police transported all five men in a police station wagon. While riding along, they sang repeatedly a beautiful Salvadoran song of gratitude to God for saving their lives. The astonished police officers asked, "How can you sing when your automobile is destroyed? And how can you be so peaceful and happy when you almost lost your lives?"

I awakened that Monday with a strange uneasiness about Paul and a strong urge to pray for him. Instead of praying, however, I spent the morning preparing some of his favorite foods. I laid down to rest after lunch. Almost immediately, I was awake and heard the ear-splitting sound of Paul's car hitting the engine of the train. I heard Paul calling, "Darling." I glanced at the night-stand clock. It read 2:13. I knew something terrible had happened and spent the next hours in deep anxiety. Paul didn't arrive home until 7:00 p.m. When I learned of the accident, I felt guilty for not praying for his safety—a lesson that has hounded me all my life.

A few weeks later in the home of missionaries Ralph and Jewel Williams in Santa Ana, El Salvador, a city 55 miles west of the accident, Paul recounted the recent calamity. The Williams' domestic servant, Angela Mancia, eagerly questioned Paul regarding the exact day and hour of his accident; she believed her amazing testimony played a part in Paul's story.

Angela wiped tears from her eyes as she told her story. "I woke up that day with a very strange uneasiness, knowing something was terribly wrong. I asked Sister Jewel for permission to go to the church to pray. In the three-block walk to the church, I invited two women friends and another two women who were cleaning the church to join me in praying for this strange burden on my heart. Not knowing for whom or what to pray, we prayed for the pastors, churches, missionaries, every department of the churches, and everything we could think of, repeating our petitions several times.

"Our knees hurt from kneeling on the hard tile floor, but the burden was so intense I asked the women to keep praying with me. All of a sudden, I sensed God had answered our prayers and we could stop praying. As we stood, one of the women looked at the church clock exclaiming, 'It's already 2:13 in the afternoon!'"

"I was almost in tears," Paul told me, "when I realized the prayers of these saintly women led by dear illiterate Angela Mancia had unquestionably saved the lives of five ministers of the gospel."

Additionally, the next year while Paul was ministering in a church in Spokane, Washington, he met a woman who said she had felt strongly impressed to pray urgently for someone by the name of Finkenbinder. Her pastor assured her there was a missionary in El Salvador by the name of Paul Finkenbinder. Obediently, this prayer warrior prayed for this unknown man at the time of the train accident.

For months Paul pondered the divine deliverance of his life; he wondered why God Himself didn't save him from harm without necessitating other's prayers. He was plagued with such questions: Is intercession necessary? God knows everything that happens to us and He is all-powerful, so why does He need somebody to intercede in prayer before He can respond to our need?

Paul remained deeply perturbed sensing God's inability to protect us unless someone prayed. He began diligently searching the Scriptures concerning God's capability and responsibility to respond to our needs. After dedicated study, he came to some logical conclusions regarding prayer intercession and prepared a sermon on the subject. Paul called his message on prayer intercession "The Paradox of the Prayer Triangle." I include here a condensed version of his studied thoughts.

"God created Adam and Eve as free moral agents, free to make choices and decisions for themselves, unlike animals born without power of choice and who obey their instincts. This free-will choice of humankind comes with the ability and responsibility to pray for our needs and desires, for God will not violate our free will unless we invite His participation.

"One biblical example is Moses when he interceded for the Israelites, who, having forgotten about God, worshipped a golden calf and obeyed their carnal nature in sexual orgies.

"God informed Moses that He planned to blot the names of the Israelites from the Book of Life for their worship of the golden calf. Moses pleaded with God for the lives of the Israelites, and as a last resort demanded that God blot his own name from the Book of Life along with his people. Moses' intercession is recorded in Psalm 106:23. *'So, he [God] said he would destroy them—had not Moses, his chosen one, stood in the breach before him to keep his wrath from destroying them.'*

"People ask, 'Did Moses change God's mind regarding the chastisement He intended for the disobedient Israelites?' Yes, I think so. The righteousness of God demanded punishment, but Moses' intercession for the Israelites changed God's mind and kept Him from destroying them.

"Another example: God said to Peter in Matthew 16:19. *'I will give you the keys of the kingdom of heaven; whatever you bind on earth will be bound in heaven, and whatever you loose on earth on earth will be loosed in heaven.'*

"This message was to Peter alone, but in Matthew 18:18, the message is to all the disciples: *'I tell you the truth, whatever you bind on earth will be bound in heaven, and whatever you loose on earth will be loosed in heaven.'*

"God, the supreme Ruler of all humankind, leaves the intercession for our needs and requests entirely up to us; He never involves Himself in our private lives, unless we invite His divine participation.

"The potential of prayer for His involvement in our lives is awesome, and the consequence of not praying for our needs is devastating!"

Chapter 9
God Used a Mule

To save Paul's life, God once endowed a mindless black mule with an instinct of imminent danger.

P aul was extremely tired after six hours on the back of a mule. Without warning or reason, his mule stubbornly refused to move. It was 10 p.m., a dark night, when Blackie, his faithful mule, stopped abruptly and refused to cross a small creek.

Blackie always responded to his commands and Paul could not understand this sudden stubbornness. He needed to gct to Apopa, the next town a few kilometers ahead. So backtracking several yards on the dirt road, Paul spurred Blackie and started out a second time. Again, the mule stopped in the same spot and refused to move.

Apprehensive of what might lie ahead but needing to get to his next mission stop, Paul went back a good distance on the road and forced Blackie into a fast gallop. Nearing the area where Blackie previously stopped, Paul spurred his usually faithful beast abnormally hard and went through the low water stream and up the road on the other side.

Within two minutes, two horsemen approached from behind, one on either side of Paul, slowing as they neared. Paul's heart pounded with loud thumps.

Paul pulled out his tiny twenty-six-inch guitar from the canvas case he carried over his shoulder. He then proceeded to greet the men. "I'm singing hymns; would you like to hear them?"

Without waiting for a response, Paul sang choruses and hymns nonstop, making up words for the songs he hadn't fully memorized. He continued playing and singing until they arrived at a tiny village.

Nearing a small, lighted shelter, one of the men suggested, "Shall we get some coffee?"

Thanking God he'd be in the company of others again, Paul dismounted Blackie, and with the two strangers close behind, they entered the dimly lit shack. Each of the three men requested coffee. Before they could take a sip of the hot brew, they heard a noisy rustling in the trees outside. It became evident that one of the men's horses was running away, so both men immediately ran outside and jumped on the remaining mare. Off they hurried after the runaway animal, liberating Paul of their undesired company.

The matronly attendant at the roadside rest stop studied Paul, a quizzical look on her weathered face. "Why are you traveling with those two evil men?"

After Paul's explanation of the riverbed experience, she shook her head in amazement. "You are a very lucky man. That dark underpass riverbed is the secret hideaway of those wicked men. They kill mercilessly for the sheer adventure of killing and for the clothing on their victims' backs."

Surely God used Blackie, an ordinary black mule, to save Paul's life, because He had more work for Paul to do.

Chapter 10
Accused of Being a Communist

Paul, a missionary in El Salvador, was accused of being a communist. This accusation almost cost him his missionary career.

Early one Sunday morning, a man of small of stature knocked at our door. He was dressed in typical Indian white pajama-style shirt and pants, with pieces of car tire fastened by twine on his dusty feet. He greeted Paul, and then asked, "Are you a missionary?"

"Yes, I am. Please, come in." Paul opened the door wide for the guest to enter and invited him to have a seat.

However, the visitor stood erect. "I am from Jicalapa. Several months ago a man from our town accepted Christ as his Savior while visiting in another city. Twelve neighbors, including myself, have met in his home every evening since then, reading the Bible he bought and learning all we can about God. But we want to know more."

Somberly intent on his mission, the Indian continued. "We believe someone can tell us more about this book and the God it talks about. I walked from Jicalapa to San Salvador to find you, because somebody told us a missionary lived here. I want to invite you to visit Jicalapa." His last words were more of a plea than a statement.

"Yes, of course, I'd be delighted to go to Jicalapa and share more of God's Word with your people," Paul replied, again offering our guest a chair. "Tell me, where is Jicalapa?"

"Jicalapa is a little town located in the department of Santa Tecla, high in the mountains of El Salvador."

After carefully noting the directions and promising to visit the new believers, Paul bid our visitor good-bye. He departed with a contented smile on his coarse, bronzed face.

A few days later, Paul and his traveling companion, Francisco Arbizú, drove to Santa Tecla, west of San Salvador, and rented mules for the 24-mile trail to Jicalapa. The mountainous path to Jicalapa was so steep in places that Paul and Arbizú had to dismount their mules and hang on to the tails of their beasts, slowly making their way up the precipitous hill.

A site along the way brought them great sorrow and a measure of curiosity. Struggling up the steep hill with a sizeable stone in his arms was a man with no legs. Jicalapa was a Catholic center where people believed miracles occurred, and since they needed a church building, a local priest required everyone coming to Jicalapa to bring a stone.

Arbizú and Paul stayed in Jicalapa several days preaching to the believers who were hungry for more of God's Word. Many people accepted Christ during that initial visit, which angered the local authorities, because they did not want evangelical missionaries establishing a church in that area. The secretary of the municipality was greatly incensed. He was in charge of the area because he was the only one who could read and write.

The local residents refused to rent to evangelical believers, so the new believers built a brush arbor for church services, which was no protection from the stones rioters threw at them.

One Sunday night, at the instigation by local authorities, soldiers disrupted the brush arbor service with machetes and clubs, taking prisoner the men in the service. Although not all were believers, the men were herded into a 10-foot by 12-foot, flea-ridden room. It had no water or toilet facilities. Their families supplied them with commodities through one small window.

Three days later, in the dark of night, the soldiers bound the men together by twos, with twine tied tightly around their thumbs. They were then forced to march 24 miles from Jutiapa to the county seat of Santa Tecla.

In prison, the Jicalapa brethren preached and sang to the other prisoners. Many inmates accepted Christ, which further angered the authorities. As punishment, the Jicalapa prisoners were denied food; however, other prisoners shared their food with them. This so infuriated the officials that they locked the Jicalapa men in solitary confinement and charged them with being Communists, a crime at that time punishable by death.

Colonel Garcia, the Santa Tecla official who hated Protestants, would not grant the prisoners freedom. In addition, because Paul had gone to Jutiapa to intercede for the men, Colonel Garcia accused Paul also of being a Communist and ordered him to leave El Salvador.

This was a serious official indictment, so for weeks Arbizú and Paul visited office after office, seeking religious freedom for the prisoners and a dismissal of the ludicrous charges against Paul.

Many weeks later, Arbizú and Paul waited at one office for several hours to speak with General Garay, the top government official. When they finally received admittance, the general was casually reading a newspaper. He appeared to have no interest in seeing them as they stood silently and politely before his desk. When he finally lifted his eyes, they introduced themselves as evangelical ministers. They stated their mission, including the charge of Communism.

General Garay greeted them kindly. "I believe you gentlemen and support what you are doing in my country, for I read my Bible every day."

General Garay called his secretary, dictated a message, and chatted with Paul and Arbizú until the typed memorandum arrived back at his desk for his signature. Then the General read his message aloud to them, adding, "Mr. Finkenbinder, I want you to deliver this to Colonel Garcia."

Paul was surprised that he personally would deliver the message ordering Colonel Garcia to free the prisoners and to drop his false charge of being a Communist.

Paul and Arbizú hurried back to Colonel Garcia. He turned pale as he read General Garay's letter, who later relieved him of his duties. He offered a two-word glum response to the two missionaries: "Message received."

Colonel Garcia lost his position. The charge against Paul was dropped, and the Jicalapa prisoners were freed. An evangelical church flourishes in Jicalapa today because a little Indian walked 30 miles from Jicalapa to San Salvador to find a missionary.

Chapter 11

The Faith of Our Daughter

*God honored the faith of a 7-year-old child, even when
her own family doubted, by healing her crossed right eye.*

The year was 1960. Paul was transmitting Bible dramas
on television every Sunday at 7:30 p.m. An evangelist
came to San Salvador to hold services in an open field close to
our home. Many people accepted Christ as their Savior. Through
faith in the Word of God, many people received healing of distinct ailments by a single prayer that the evangelist offered to
God.

For our family one healing was significant: the divine healing
of Ellin, our 7-year-old daughter, who had a crossed right eye.
The eye began crossing when she was four. At the time of her
healing she was wearing her second pair of corrective glasses;
her ophthalmologist had predicted surgery as the next course of
action.

The evangelist (I will keep him unidentified as explained by
details that follow) shared dinner with us in our home the day he
arrived in San Salvador. Ellin, our youngest child, inquired about
our visitor, so I explained he was an evangelist who would tell
people about Jesus and pray for their healing.

"Oh, goody!" Our petite first-grader jumped up and down and clapped her hands. "God will heal me and I won't have to wear these awful glasses."

Positive that God was going to heal her, Ellin ran and skipped around the house, singing joyfully as though it were Christmas and she were going to receive every gift on her list.

Evening came and Ellincita, as we called her, sat excitedly beside me on the platform while her daddy interpreted the evangelist's message. After the stimulating message regarding God's promises, the evangelist instructed the parents to place their hands on their children, or on their own bodies, in the place that needed healing. I feared my lack of faith could nullify Ellin's implicit faith, so I held her glasses while my little girl put a tiny hand over each eye.

After the prayer she looked at me with tear-brimmed eyes and nervously reached for her glasses. She leaned toward me and whispered, "Tomorrow I won't have to wear the glasses, will I, Mommy?"

After the prayer, Ellin's right eye was still halfway behind her nose, appearing as crossed as before; however, her countenance radiated with the anticipation of complete healing. She truly believed she would never have to use her glasses again. I didn't have her faith and felt unintelligent as I blurted out, "Why not, Ellin?"

"Why not?" Her voice raised in indignation at my apparent unawareness of her healed eye. With absolute confidence she declared, "Because God has healed me."

Choking with tears and diverse emotions tumbling in my heart, I was apprehensive of damaging Ellin's faith. I diplomatically responded, "Of course, if God healed you, you won't have to wear your glasses."

Ellin radiated assurance of God's answered prayer. "Then I'll take the glasses off now, Mommy. It's a shame we didn't bring the case to carry them home in." With an air of finality, she handed me her tiny pink-rimmed glasses, as though she were ridding herself of burdensome material she would never use again.

Paul and I were totally perplexed at our daughter's confidence that her right eye had been fully healed; her eye was still behind her nose and appeared as cross-eyed as ever.

Early the next morning before breakfast, without her glasses, Ellin ran up and down the sidewalk in front of our house, excitedly exclaiming, "God operated on my eye and didn't even use a knife."

Embarrassed before our neighbors, Paul and I wondered what we should do. Ellin's eye was still crossed, but one thing was different: She had absolutely no pain. The family spent an exasperating week because Ellin refused to wear her glasses to school, which embarrassed her siblings.

At the dinner table Wednesday noon, Paul suggested to Ellin, "Perhaps you should attend another evangelistic service. You might need another touch from God."

She heaved a big sigh. Exasperation covered her face and tainted her tone. She looked at her father. "Daddy, do you mean God can't heal me at home?"

"W-w-well, yes, Honey, God can heal you at home." His Adam's apple bobbled as he gulped. He repeatedly wiped his hands on his napkin. His embarrassment at his feeble faith was evident.

"Okay, I'll stay home then, because I have to get up early to go to school." Ellin left the table and exited the room, leaving the family stunned and speechless.

Saturday, while I brushed Ellin's hair in preparation for that evening's service, I casually asked, "Ellin, what are you going to do when the evangelist prays for the sick?"

Ellin straightened her tiny body, looked straight into my face, with her little crossed eye still appearing the same. "Mommy, you want me to ask Jesus to heal me, but He already did that. I'm going tonight to thank Him."

Ellin walked out of the bathroom, leaving me with her hairbrush in my hand. I stood there overwhelmed with the truth that my daughter understood and accepted God's promises more than I did. I couldn't stop the tears as I begged God's forgiveness for my unbelief, accepted Ellin's healing from that moment, and praised Him for the healing miracle.

Within a month, Ellin's right eye straightened completely to its correct position, leaving a reminder of God's goodness and our child's simple faith, a tiny pair of pink-framed glasses that she never used again.

But this story didn't end there.

Our daughter's miraculous healing, didn't quite prepare us for the lesson God had reserved for us.

Paul's Church in Your Home telecasts enjoyed in all El Salvador on Sunday nights from 7:30 to 8 p.m. commanded a large amount of attention. He usually picked up the evangelist at his hotel after his Sunday night television program to take him to the open park crusade service. However, the last Sunday of the crusade, Paul decided to take the evangelist to the television station to see a live drama program in action. Without advising the evangelist of his plans, Paul went to the hotel before the television program and was astonished to find him in the bar, sitting with a woman and drinks in front of them.

Dumbfounded, perplexed, scandalized, and confused, Paul exited the hotel without the evangelist's seeing him. God mercifully helped him disregard the evangelist incident and serenely present the live telecast with a concluding message of Christ's offer of salvation.

When the television program ended, Paul returned to the hotel. The evangelist, with his Bible in hand, waited for Paul in the lobby. Fighting revolting nausea, Paul declined to speak of the incident and without enthusiasm interpreted the evangelist's message into Spanish.

After the evening service, Paul, the evangelist, and I sat in the car. Paul confronted the evangelist, who vehemently denied everything. Paul locked his gaze on the face of the insolent evangelist, declaring he knew what he saw and would be reporting him to the crusade executive committee. The man broke down in tears. After two hours in what appeared to be genuine repentance, he gave a penitent and remorseful prayer. We left him at the hotel.

The evangelistic services were ending Wednesday, so Paul kept this entire incident to himself, not wanting to disrupt the faith of thousands of people.

Paul agonized as he anxiously sought answers to tormenting questions: How God could possibly use a man effectively in evangelism when his personal testimony did not measure up to God's Word. How could and why did God heal sick people, including our daughter, through the prayers of a hypocritical minister of the gospel of Jesus Christ? What does God say about the personal salvation of a minister of the gospel who does not live according to God's holy standards? Does God utilize ethically immoral ministers to fulfill His purposes on earth?

The Bible says that the fear of God is the beginning of wisdom (Prov. 1:7). After months of studying the Scriptures, Paul concluded that God always honors His Word. God saves people from eternal damnation and heals our bodies because Jesus gave his life for that purpose, no matter who makes the proclamation.

Without the anointing of the Holy Spirit a man or woman can preach the gospel with apparent success—but only for a time before ultimately failing.

A year later, this evangelist, through whom many people, including our own daughter, were healed, left his faithful wife of many years. He had become a sad, lost alcoholic.

Paul further explained: "A giant flywheel will continue to whirl around even after being disconnected from the power source. In time, the centrifugal force will lessen and ultimately come to a stop, just as a minister's blessing will end if He is not connected to God."

God always honors His Word. He saves people from eternal damnation and heals the sick through faith in the sacrifice and death of Jesus Christ.

Chapter 12
Total Surrender

God demanded we make the total surrender
of our five children.

By 1958 radio was the fulfilling delight of Paul's 15-year missionary career in El Salvador. The radio programs, which started in July 1955, resonated in several Central and South American countries. Preparing and recording the 15-minute daily "The Church of the Air" broadcasts and duplicating them for other stations was an enormous task, but Paul never tired of the chore. In fact, in anticipation of our yearlong furlough, he produced and recorded programs to cover the entire time he would be away from El Salvador.

We were the proud parents of five children. Our two sons were already studying in the United States, and our three daughters were living with us in El Salvador. They were terrified at the prospect of leaving El Salvador, the country of their birth, and living in a foreign land called America. After much deliberation, we decided that it would be prudent to take a temporary leave of absence from El Salvador and devote time to our children. Secretly Paul and I planned to leave El Salvador in July and live with our children for an indefinite time in the United States.

In March 1958 we attended the biannual missionary retreat in Guatemala City where missionaries of our denomination from all of Central America gathered. From the moment we arrived, both of us were impressed with an underlying message that God did not want us to remain in the United States after our year furlough. Every message, every conversation, and every song we heard was like a broken record saying, "Don't go home now. Don't go home now."

This disturbing message came to us constantly, and since our family plans were secretive, it was apparent that the messages were from God. They were unrelenting and intense, reducing both Paul and me to tears. Sensing our turmoil, our colleagues surrounded us daily and prayed for us numerous times.

Deciding against residency in the United States with our daughters as we had promised them brought us face-to-face with the most important and hardest decision of our lives! We felt like Abraham when he was asked to sacrifice his son Isaac. Paul recognized that as the mother I would experience the greatest pain of sending the children one by one to the care of others in the United States, so he left the final decision entirely with me.

Furthermore, I was painfully conscious that Paul's entire future hinged on the call God put on his heart when he was still at Zion. I felt the weight and the responsibility of the whole world on my shoulders because Paul's ministry depended on my decision.

By the end of the missionary retreat in Guatemala City, independently we both realized that God's peace was impossible to obtain without surrendering to Him our most precious earthly possessions. Humbly we surrendered our wills to God, promising to return to El Salvador after our furlough and to trust Him implicitly for the welfare of our children. When we submitted our wills and said, "Lord, we'll return to El Salvador and trust you for the future welfare of our children," we felt an incredible peace in our hearts, even though the tears remained.

We opened the Bible to continue our daily Bible reading from the previous day. These words in Matthew 19:29 ministered to our hearts: *"And everyone who has left houses or brothers or sisters or mother or father or children or fields for my sake will receive a hundred times as much and will inherit eternal life."* It appeared that God inserted those reassuring words in the Holy Scriptures just for us.

"Lord," we proclaimed simultaneously, "we trust You with our children and praise You for the promise of eternal life and the hundredfold blessing that we request to be in souls."

God gave us joy and peace as we gave our five children to Him and received His promise of a hundredfold blessing. Today, all five of our children love and serve the Lord. What better heritage to leave than this?

Chapter 13
Marital Adjustments

Paul says he fell in love with me the first time he saw me while we were both students at Zion Bible Institute in November 1940.

"I've never stopped loving Linda; however, I took her for granted, devouring her devotion and affection without responding in like fashion to her loving servitude. I was a good Latino husband, macho and demanding, expecting her to be one with me without accepting her as a companion in ministry."

Paul believed that the marriage certificate made us one flesh, and he anticipated that I would think and speak like him, believing this oneness came automatically.

Paul is of German descent, born and reared in Puerto Rico by missionary parents. There he learned Spanish and the Latin culture, which taught to always present a polite, courteous front, and cautiously allow people to save face. Paul is kind, happy, and always "on top of the world," with above average ethical morality and extraordinary intellectual judgment. The personality I saw when I married Paul was a charming, ambitious, perfectionist youth with the aspiration to be a missionary in God's service.

I am also of German Dutch decent, the daughter of ex-Amish farmers whose manner of speech is honest but blunt and straightforward, which presented us with challenges in our marriage.

I did not have the happy childhood that Paul had. My strict, demanding father was harsh and often cruel, never permitting me self-expression or self-confidence. If we children wanted to go out with friends for an evening, our father always insisted we get up earlier the next morning without complaining as a compensation for pleasure. Of course, I took all my insecurities and gloominess into marriage. I couldn't help but feel envious of Paul's happy disposition and upbringing.

The language difference presents an example of the marriage adjustments we made. Neither one of us confidently communicated clearly because of the language distinction, although we didn't initially realize this was a major problem. Nevertheless, Paul and I seldom fought angrily—or went to sleep in anger—since serving God was our primary purpose in life; we resolved our differences amicably. Both of us can honestly report that we argued, sometimes loudly, but never screaming in unrestrained anger.

One day during our first year of marriage, seeing a well-worn Spanish First Grade Reader in a second-hand store, Paul snatched it and with a big smile waved it in front of me. "Linda, this is what you need to learn Spanish! Let's buy it."

Since Spanish was Paul's first language, he confidently supposed teaching me Spanish would be a simple undertaking. "After all," he reasoned, "in Spanish, each of the five vowels has only one pronouncement, so Linda should pronounce Spanish words easily."

That evening sitting at our kitchen table, Paul pointed out the five vowels: A-E-I-O-U. He sounded out each Spanish vowel several times, explaining that these vowels always have the same sound. Then, just like that, without first reading the foreign words to me, Paul insisted I attempt to read a page of Spanish words based only on the vowel sounds he had "taught" me. Shy, unwilling to appear unintelligent, and not having retained the sounds of the vowels and thus unable to pronounce Spanish words, I thought Paul insensitive to ask me to try.

"Linda, if you want to learn Spanish, you must start to speak it."

I refused to repeat the words unless he pronounced them first.

We sat quietly for one whole hour in a silence that became more pronounced with each passing moment. We both diplomatically evaded an argument. Finally, with a submissive sigh, Paul closed the Spanish reader, and without either of us mentioning the failed endeavor, we went to bed.

The next evening we had another identical lesson, only this class lasted an hour and a half. To Paul, I was an impossible student, hopelessly fated not to learn Spanish. I, on the other hand, definitely felt unimpressed with my husband's teaching skills.

For years, Paul had the bizarre habit of banging his toothbrush on the edge of the washbasin for several seconds after brushing his teeth, playing some kind of melodic rhythm. This annoying banging accompaniment to his melody drove me crazy.

I irritated Paul by carelessly squeezing our tube of toothpaste in the middle, instead of from the bottom.

He scolded me repeatedly, but I was an extremely busy mother of five small children, schoolteacher to three, and I felt privileged to have time to brush my teeth.

One day we were both in the bathroom together. Paul was doing his customary toothbrush-banging symphony and offering his lecture on my incorrectly squeezing the toothpaste. That's all it took for the floodgate of tears to overtake me. "I wish I could die so you would miss me and want me here to squeeze your dumb toothpaste," I said.

Paul made no comment regarding my outburst of obvious discontent, but that was the last time he scolded me for squeezing the toothpaste. And to his credit he discontinued banging his toothbrush on the washbasin.

We remember those lessons frequently and thank God that we disagreed without using offensive words or displaying angry looks. Shamefully and sadly, we didn't carry the respect principle throughout our whole marriage, because as Paul admits, he was too particular and demanding.

Our two sons, Paul and Gene, followed by three daughters, Sharon, Joan, and Ellin, within the first 10 years of our marriage, filled our home with demanding but pleasurable activity. Paul and I agreed on the children's discipline and never permitted a child to obtain permission from one of us when the other had refused it. We always had family devotions together after breakfast, which included memorizing portions of Scripture and even whole chapters of the Bible.

For entertainment in El Salvador, we missionaries loved to go to Lake Ilopango or Coatepeque or to the ocean for picnics and swimming. Often we joined with the Stewart and Lindvall families for a day of leisure. Sometimes in the evenings, we drove up a mountainside to watch Izalco, our active volcano, erupt every few moments. It was exciting to see red-hot lava spew and flow down the growing mountain cone. Even from a half-mile distance, we could feel the heat.

Paul says that when we married, he was aware of my insecurities and wanted to love, care for, and console me. He always assured me that his love was unconditional, for love has nothing to do with everyday misunderstandings or disagreements. It took years and a special incident for me to believe the certainty of Paul's love that he freely demonstrated regardless of my misgivings.

Most of the time Paul wasn't conscious of my personal needs. It was as though he divorced himself from me and married his ministry, leaving me in charge of the children. I reflected my un-happiness with my countenance and cross words.

One hot, extremely humid morning, I waited for Paul to give me his customary hug when he returned from the post office, but this day he failed to hug me. The tedious task of schooling three of our children and doing laundry while preparing dinner was difficult to say the least. I needed Paul's moral support. When he continued with other activities, seemingly oblivious to his apparent lack of affection and my needing an extra measure of it, I harbored the thought that he was tired of me and I was not the wife he wanted.

This unhealthy concept exacerbated in my mind all day. When we retired that evening, Paul, weary from the heat and his work anxieties, went right to sleep. His falling asleep immediately reinforced my foolish fears and my mind ran wild with the dread that Paul was thinking amorously of someone else.

At 2:00 in the morning, overcome with insecurity and suspicions, I decided to speak with Paul and learn why he had neglected me when he returned from the post office. Sobbing, I nudged Paul's arm. When he grunted a response, I informed him he had hurt my feelings that morning. Immediately, Paul wrapped me in his arms, begging my forgiveness, apologizing for hurting my feelings, and assuring me that he loved me very much. Repeatedly Paul reassured me of his love until I became peaceful. Then as he turned over to go back to sleep he asked, "By the way, Hon, what did I do?"

What love! I felt ridiculous for being critical of him when he was completely innocent of any wrongdoing. Paul taught me an enormous lesson with his kind, loving, uncritical, non-scolding attitude, and his reassuring words of unconditional love.

I adored Paul in spite of his machismo and greatly admired his ministry, but I felt slighted in the home and disappointed that

77

I wasn't part of his ministry life. We had been married 15 years, and I complained repeatedly because everything was for man's enjoyment.

What I really sought from Paul were words of appreciation for my work as mother of his five children and gratitude for my contribution to our marriage. Paul didn't realize that with words of appreciation he could change my complaints to happiness. Instead of compliments, he instructed me in how to do my work more efficiently.

One day when I began to complain, instead of being irritated or walking away and leaving me alone, Paul kindly said, "Hon, we didn't make the marriage rules that have always been here, so why don't you check the Bible for answers to your questions?"

Serving God was my only desire, so I accepted the Bible-reading challenge and began reading in Genesis. Almost immediately, I noted God's chastisement of Eve in Genesis 3:16: "Thy desire shall be to thy husband" (KJV). The biblical message was clear that God had chosen the man as the head of the home. I groaned aloud at its implication, but at the same time I realized I couldn't change the Word of God. So I continued reading.

The story of Abraham and Sarah fascinated me, and I read it repeatedly for two weeks before I understood the lesson God wanted me to learn. Sarah respected Abraham, and I realized that even though Paul didn't pay attention to me, I was guilty of not respecting him. I began demonstrating the respect Paul rightly deserved, and he began to pay more attention to me. I began to listen to him, to speak more politely to him, to admire him and to take notice of his plans and desires. This change bettered our marriage, and even though Paul was unconscious of the respect principle I applied, we both enjoyed the effects.

My ambition was to serve God, although I lacked the talents Paul had. I decided that Paul would be my ministry, and if I couldn't help him in a project, I wouldn't hinder. I prayed constantly for his efforts and cooperated with him in every way I could.

At that time there were no marriage seminars, marriage counselors, or marriage books, but since God was first in our lives, He helped us. Paul's activities with the youth movement, teaching in the Bible school, and visiting churches nearly every weekend did not give us time to focus on our marital necessities.

God taught me to respect and honor Paul, an important lesson for a happy marriage, because God made the woman as man's helpmate.

Chapter 14
Winning Professional People to Christ

*For many years, the missionaries in El Salvador sought ways
to establish friendships with professionals that they might tell
them that the gospel of Jesus Christ was also for them.
The circumstances that guided Paul to fulfill this ambitious
undertaking were amazing.*

We lived next door to a fine-furniture factory. Paul visited
often with Carlos Vides, the owner. One Thanksgiving
Day Carlos's wife, Julia, prepared a special turkey banquet for
the employees. Knowing Paul was a religious minister, Carlos
invited Paul to speak to his workers. Paul's message emphasized
the need of having a personal relationship with God. After his
talk, Paul noticed Carlos' indifference to the message, so Paul
expressed to Carlos that the message was for him also.

"Oh, no." Carlos shook his head, and then pointed toward his
employees. "These men need it, not me."

Paul's Puerto Rican heritage allowed him to understand this
strange opinion Carlos held. "In Spanish-speaking countries, a
powerful dominating racial caste system reigns, tracing back to
the monarchs and royal classes of Europe. This highly socialized
caste system has never experienced the sense of equality that per-
vades our American way of life. The consideration that all men
are created equal, a cornerstone of American democracy, is

largely alien to most Latin American countries. This social order is so ingrained within the traditions that even the Spanish language reflects the difference in the social classes."

One example of this peculiar diversity is in the usage of the English word *you*, which has two forms of usage in Spanish—*tu* and *usted*. *Tu* is the expression one uses in conversation to God, a close friend, and a child; strangely, in speaking to an animal *tu* is an informal word. *Usted*, on the other hand, is the formal usage used in speaking to a stranger, one's supervisor, or in any situation that calls for a treatment of respect or deference. It would never occur to a landowner to speak to a person of the working class using *usted*. In like manner, the worker would politely converse with the landowner using *usted*, never using the *tu* form. This is the custom.

This peculiar disparity of language greatly affects the propagation of the gospel of Jesus Christ in Spanish-speaking countries. Evangelization in Latin America until the decades of the 40s and 50s was almost entirely among the poor: the *tu*s. The more educated people have been outside the range of the gospel, because they believed something for the uneducated and underprivileged was certainly not for them.

Paul's burden was to reach that unreached segment of society: the political leaders, scientists, scholars, educators and military authorities. So he offered himself to God. "God, I offer myself to be your witness to the social class of the Republic."

Religion is a big part of the lives of the Salvadorans, but most of the men attend only weddings, baby baptisms, and Easter and Christmas celebrations. In theory, Catholics are very devout, but mostly without a personal relationship with Jesus Christ. It was many years before we had the opportunity to generate friendship with people of the upper class.

Paul made friends with Ernesto MacEntee (Neco), a coffee plantation owner. One day Neco invited Paul to a special gathering at a local hotel, but he didn't want to tell Paul, even though Paul insisted, what kind of gathering it was.

"I'd prefer not tell you, Pablo, but I'm confident you will find the evening interesting and enjoyable." Neco flashed a kind smile.

Immediately upon entering the hotel room with Neco, Paul was pleasantly impressed with a gathering of 40 professional men and women. Excited, he observed a group of socialites, the populace with whom he most wanted to befriend and share the gospel of Jesus Christ.

Paul became so enthralled with the prospect of touching bases with these Dale Carnegie professionals; he borrowed $160 and signed up that night for the 13-week Dale Carnegie Leadership Training Course. This exceptional public-speaking course gives training for timed discourses, from one or more minutes, based on descriptions of personal life experience or training. In this course one cannot address politics or religion, but Paul determined this wouldn't hinder him from making friends—something he eagerly looked forward to.

The application the course drummed into everyone is never to make a point without telling a story and never to tell a story without making a point. This was considered essential information in preparing a discourse.

After completing the Dale Carnegie Course, Paul remained with the group as a Graduate Assistant. Then he declared, "If I am going to reach these people for Christ, I need Linda."

He borrowed another $160 and I joined the new group of 40 people; all this was done in preparation for our next step in evangelizing Salvadoran professionals.

The Dale Carnegie Leadership Training Course became our contact leading to associations and friendships with the professionals in El Salvador, which then allowed us to tell them of Christ.

After completing the leadership-training course, Paul rented the small Union Church, where North American embassy personnel worshipped on Sundays, to hold services on Friday nights.

Our churches use hymnbooks with only the words, so Paul bought a dozen hymnals with both words and music. He hired an organist instead of involving another missionary who didn't share our vision. Paul was overjoyed when 12 of our Carnegie friends responded to our invitation and attended the first Friday night service in the Union Church.

Paul selected the page number of a hymn, gave the signal for the organist to play the introduction, and anticipated the attendees joining him in singing. To his consternation and disappointment, he found himself singing alone! Discouraged, he valiantly encouraged everyone to join him on the chorus, but no one responded. Paul continued with a second and third song, determinedly singing all three verses of each song—and wanting to drop through the floor, for he was the only one singing.

The tension eased as he presented an illustrated message using 10 small clay flowerpots representing the Ten Commandments God gave to Moses.

To illustrate how the human race has broken each commandment, one by one Paul broke each flowerpot and put the shattered pieces into a large ornate clay jar that represented Christ.

To illustrate Christ's death on the cross, Paul shattered the large ornate jar that contained the shattered Ten Commandments, causing the group to gasp. His message ended with the presentation of another identical large clay jar representing the risen Christ.

It was a beautiful Easter presentation and everyone seemed to enjoy it, although the spiritual message of the cross seemingly made no impression on the audience.

Paul invited the group to return the next week, but only three people attended the meetings on the next two Fridays. Following the custom of some churches, Paul sang three songs in each service.

Neco, the friend who invited Paul to the Dale Carnegie Leadership Training Course, approached Paul after the third Friday night service with a complaint. "Paul, we don't want to sing, we came to hear you speak."

Paul kindly thanked Neco, but he dismissed his friend's viewpoint. Paul believed he was the professional in church affairs, not Neco.

We returned home from that Friday night gathering totally defeated. Our evangelism efforts to win our Carnegie friends to Christ were unproductive. We retired in silence. Paul faked sleep; but at 2 a.m., unable to disregard our dilemma any longer, I cautiously suggested, "Hon, shall we pray about the Friday night service?"

"Pray about what?" Paul's answer seemed to indicate he had the whole thing under control, even though it was obvious he was totally defeated in spirit.

"Let's ask God for divine guidance concerning this upper-class evangelism effort," I implored.

Paul agreed, so we knelt beside our bed and humbly admitted our failure in this new venture to reach out to professionals. We asked God for divine direction.

After prayer, Paul went to sleep. That night he dreamed he was in Israel 2,000 years ago when Jesus delivered what we refer to as the Sermon on the Mount. In his dream, Paul nudged the man on his right and then another on his left, regarding Jesus' not singing hymns before His message. When they paid no attention to him, Paul determined to complain to Jesus about the oversight, but while walking toward Him, he awoke feeling indescribably stupid.

The dream made Paul realize that the singing customs in our evangelical services were normal to us, but he had failed to take into account that these people did not have a song in their hearts.

Paul dismissed the organist and told Neco there would be no more singing; however, he was too embarrassed to tell him about the dream. The next Friday, Paul began the service without preliminary singing, which was difficult for him at first.

One Friday night a neighbor, Doris Mencía, prayed to surrender her heart to God. A few weeks later, she questioned Paul if it was appropriate to kneel to accept Christ. Her actions surprised us until we realized that her first acceptance was intellectual while the second time she felt the inspiration of God's offer—a reaction we have noted by other *usted* people.

Doris Mencía's life as a mistress to a businessman in San Salvador, with whom she mothered two sons, changed dramatically. In reading God's Word, Doris realized she was living in sin; so she cut off all contact and personal support from him. Doris currently lives in Florida near her married lawyer and architect sons; all serve God and are vibrant in their testimony of God's grace.

Jorge and Magda were part of the Friday night group. One day Magna asked, "Do you mean you have been in El Salvador for 19 years and this is the first time we are hearing this good news of salvation?"

This face-to-face indictment was distressing to hear and even more painful to respond to. "We needed to befriend you before sharing the gospel of Jesus Christ. The Carnegie Course was the first opportunity we had to meet you," was the only explanation we could give her.

Several of the Friday-night group considered our get-togethers a social activity for fellowship only. They enjoyed hearing God's Word but were wary of a personal relationship with God; they did not believe it of importance to them personally.

When we returned to the United States to live in August 1964, we were confident of the salvation of only two of our Carnegie contacts; however, the group wanted to continue meeting, so missionaries John and Lois Bueno accepted the responsibility to guide them. Countless times, the Buenos became disheartened and nearly gave up trying to evangelize this social group. Later, the weekly socialites met on Tuesday nights, sometimes for a dinner, although the group continued to be "The Friday night group that meets on Tuesday."

The Carlos Valiente family, proprietors of a prestigious costume jewelry shop in San Salvador, began another Christian get-together after The Church in Your Home telecasts started in 1960. The group met on Sundays in a hall Carlos Valiente rented; he named the gathering Josue (Joseph). In time, after we left the country in 1964, our "Friday night group" united with this gathering and together they became the renowned Josue Church.

This merger in July 1984 kept the Josue name; many middle- and upper-class people, including lawyers, doctors, and political leaders, such as a past vice president of El Salvador, attend.

Our last report in 1995 of the 2,000-member Josue Church is that it had 500 students studying in its English-speaking primary school. The congregation had established nine new churches and is sending and supporting missionaries in several parts of the world.

Our professional friends from Dale Carnegie Leadership Training Course now know the salvation that Jesus offers.

Chapter 15

Does God Still Reveal Himself to Humankind?

God revealed Jesus to Gustavo's religious auntie.

Gustavo Galdámez was a devout Roman Catholic. He attended private schools and studied several years in a convent in preparation for the priesthood. He became incredulous and disheartened when he observed morally erroneous indiscretions in the convent. Discouraged and disillusioned, he discontinued his studies and roamed El Salvador and Guatemala as an infidel. For several years, he reasoned that if there is no God in the Catholic Church, there is no God at all.

During Gustavo's disenchanted wanderings, he received word that his auntie, who had proudly sponsored his studies in the El Salvador convent, was ill, so he hurried home.

Gustavo's auntie was wholly dedicated and loyal to the predominant religion of the Republic and attended Mass daily. Her room was a virtual shrine, displaying a number of large images of saints, burning candles, and fragrant incense.

Several times his auntie dreamed that Jesus Himself had appeared to her and explained that the idols, candles, and incense in her room were not necessary for her salvation; He told her that she needed only to believe in Him. However, at her insistence to remove the worship items from her room, the family and her confessing priest became greatly distressed. That's when they sent for Gustavo.

The family was certain Gustavo's training in the convent would enable him to convince his auntie regarding the disposal of her idols. Nevertheless, Gustavo did not understand when his auntie excitedly told him about her repeated dreams. He agreed with the family that she should keep them.

"But, Gustavo," the older woman exclaimed, "Jesus not only told me I didn't need these idols, He gave me Living Water and told me I didn't need anything else."

Her words and earnestness left Gustavo speechless.

At his auntie's continued insistence to remove the shrine from her room, the family priest concluded that she was mentally unstable; therefore, they might as well do as she requested. Consequently, the family removed all the worship objects. Gustavo's auntie died peacefully.

Her serene death greatly affected Gustavo, since she didn't appear to be out of her mind and she had absolutely no fear of death—something that Gustavo greatly feared.

A few weeks after his auntie's death, Gustavo was traveling along the banks of a river. He came unexpectedly upon the water baptismal service of evangelical believers. He observed the scene: a large crowd of happy dedicated Christians, the singing and preaching; the water immersion, and a man's testimony of how God had changed his life. This man's obvious joy and peace reminded Gustavo of his auntie's peace; Gustavo also remembered her testimony about Jesus.

This chance encounter of the water baptismal service eventually led to Gustavo's own salvation in Jesus Christ. The peace in his heart he had longed for and never experienced in the convent was now his. At first Gustavo devoured the Bible alone, then he enrolled in Templo Betel, the Assemblies of God Bible school in Santa Ana, El Salvador. He was pastor of a few churches; in time Gustavo became pastor of Templo Betel church. Because of his prominence, in 1957 he became the third superintendent of our denomination in El Salvador. He traveled the country on a small motorcycle.

Many people ask, "Is God real?" "Is He sovereign?" "Does He still reveal Himself to humankind?" "How can we know Him personally?" "What about people of other languages, or those who live in remote villages, who have never had an opportunity to hear the gospel message? Can they know God?"

This testimony of Gustavo Galdámez reveals the power and the great love of God. In Gustavo's words, he declares, "I know I will meet my auntie in heaven because she partook of Jesus' 'Living Water.'"

The light of God's Word reached his auntie's heart, and she recognized Him as her Savior.

One day while Paul and Brother Galdámez were resting in their hammocks in Tacuba, El Salvador, Paul started strumming on his 26-inch guitar that he took on his travels. As the men relaxed and Paul played his guitar, he penned words and music to "Esclavo" ("I Was a Slave to Sin"), one of six songs that Paul wrote in El Salvador. It is a beautiful song about a sinner who lived in despair, without hope and condemned to die, but Christ paid his debt that the sinner had no way of paying. The chorus is simple but profound: "Now I am free and God will never let me fall from His arms of love, and He truly loves me." Of course, this is the translated version, but in Spanish, it is beautifully poetic.

Chapter 16
"A Message to the Conscience" Program is Born

A "Message to the Conscience" was born—a new format and name for Hermano Pablo's radio program.

"Hermano Pablo, when your 15-minute radio program comes on at 6:45 in the morning, the station loses listeners," Raul Monson, director of programming of YSU told Paul.

"The radio station doesn't want to lose listeners; neither do I. What can I do?"

"Put the program on at four o'clock in the afternoon, when the little old ladies can listen to a long monologue about God?" Monson suggested.

Paul ignored the derogatory comment about his 15-minute radio program but paid attention to the program director's suggestion. Interestingly, Monson typified the man whose whole interests in life were liquor, women, and wealth. And he was precisely the type of man Paul aspired to reach with the gospel of Jesus Christ.

"Raul, I don't want another hour; there has to be another solution."

"Well, yes, there is, Hermano Pablo, but you won't like it."

Paul was immediately curious, enthralled with the possibility of exploring any new challenge. "Try me, Raul."

"Make a micro program." Raul studied Paul for his reaction.

Paul's brows knit together. "Micro? How micro should it be?" There were no micro programs being done at this time.

"Three or four minutes."

"Raul, it's impossible to condense my radio messages to four minutes when I have difficulty conveying all I have on my heart in 15 minutes."

"Bring me any of your taped radio programs and I'll condense them to four minutes. You can judge for yourself that I won't take anything essential out of it."

Paul was conscious of Raul's disapproval of his radio programs, but he realized the program director made a valuable point.

"Let me consider your idea for a couple weeks, Raul." The men shook hands and said good-bye.

Paul returned to the YSU radio station two weeks later. He offered a counter proposal. "Raul, I'll make the change you suggested on two conditions."

"What two conditions do you want?"

"First, I want three, five-minute spots of radio time for my present 15-minute segment and for the same price."

"That's impossible, Hermano Pablo. With three different broadcast times, you are speaking to three different audiences, which necessitates triple charges. But what is the second condition?"

"You are the professional in radio broadcasting, so I need your help with the format of the micro program."

"Because you will permit me to assist you with the new program, I will alter your present contract to three different spots a day for the same price. The first thing we have to do is change the name of the broadcast."

The set of his jaw let Paul know that Raul was emphatic about changing the program name. Appreciative of the new price arrangement, however Paul was bewildered at Raul's criticism of the program name. "What's wrong with 'The Church of the Air' name?"

"To begin with, no one is interested in church, and everybody knows you are on the air."

Paul was astonished that any person would be offended by church, and then he realized that Raul, "the fish," was telling him, "the fisherman," what bait not to use to catch him. "Then what shall I call the new program?"

Raul deliberated for possibly 20 seconds before responding. "Call it 'A Message to the Conscience', because that is the message your programs convey."

Raul's selection of a name appealed to Paul immediately. "'A Message to the Conscience' is a brilliant title."

"And if you wouldn't mind, Hermano Pablo, I'd like to make the introduction and conclusion on your program."

"Magnificent, Raul! I'd appreciate your contribution. Your voice would be an attraction to the program."

So together Paul and Raul put together a 10-second opening to the new radio program, starting with "'A Message to the Conscience', a moment of reflection in your daily life, in the voice of Hermano Pablo," underscored with the music of the hymn "Great Is Thy Faithfulness."

Paul decided that every radio program would begin with a short story about the problems all people face: adultery, abortion, infidelity, suicide, and more. Each anecdote would conclude with God's promise to solve our problems.

Paul's target audience was to be the adult male, between the ages of 25 and 50, a businessperson, egocentric, and interested only in the pleasures of this life. The message would need to be positive, would not use religious terminology or political themes, and would never ask for contributions. Every day Paul would relate a parable like Jesus did: "A man went from Jerusalem to Jericho . . ." and would end with a life-changing moral application, pointing to God, the solution to their problems.

Changing from the free-style 15-minute radio programs to one with only four minutes would have been a difficult challenge if Paul hadn't taken the Dale Carnegie Leadership Course the year before. The application of "Never make a point without telling a story" and "Never tell a story without making a point" was the perfect blueprint he needed for his new program. At the same time, a communication is intelligent, interesting, and memorable if 20 percent of the words used are objects, dates, numbers, or names of people. This change in May 1964 from a 15-minute to a four-minute format, with a new name, increased correspondence from nonbelievers by 50 percent.

The new micro "A Message to the Conscience" radio program, the first micro program in Latin America, became even more popular in propagating the gospel to Hispanic people.

Chapter 17
Live Television

Paul learned that accomplishing great exploits for God is entirely man's option to accept or reject. Obsessed with the desire to reach the Salvadoran people for Christ without experience or necessary funds, Paul took advantage of the open door of television.

L ate in 1959, black-and-white television came to El Salvador. Paul saw that the politicians, lawyers, doctors, and other professional people he wanted to reach with the gospel owned television sets. He determined to use that medium to preach the gospel.

"My desire," he said, "is to point my finger at the president of El Salvador and tell him that he needs to accept Jesus as His Savior."

He had absolutely no television experience, much less money, but Paul knew he'd capture everyone's attention if he could just get in front of the television cameras. YSU, the radio station he had broadcast on for five years, introduced television into the country. Paul lived at the television station for days at a time, as he had before he started his radio program. He absorbed every detail of production, from the control rooms to the staged product.

Totally enthralled by the opportunity television provided for preaching the gospel—money or not—in 1960 Paul went to the television station manager and requested a contract for a program titled "The Church in Your Home". All the details in the contract appeared to be normal: the time was Sunday evening, 7:30 to 8:00 p.m., a perfect time because most Salvadoran people go to the beaches on Sunday and return in the late afternoon. The manager had set the length of the contract at one year, which was customary for his radio broadcast contracts. However, Paul was terrified at committing to a year, because the production costs and station time, unlike radio that cost $133 a month, would be $300 a week, an enormous amount to contemplate.

Confronted with this doubt, Paul's heart cried, "God, shall I sign this television contract or not?" Praying and deliberating how he would obtain the money, he waited for the usual euphoric feeling demonstrating it was God's will. But the euphoria never came. Yet, the eerie impression of a bucket of cold water pouring over him—indicating it was not God's will—didn't occur either.

His heart determined to know God's direction. Paul feared making a wrong decision. "God, guide me. I can't make this decision alone."

But God in heaven was silent.

Finally, the silence became a message that distinctly impressed Paul that God had left the decision to sign or not to sign the contract entirely up to him.

"Lord, this is too much responsibility for me alone. Where will I get $300 a week?"

Paul sensed God's compassion. "Son, you don't have to sign the television contract."

Rationalizing his deep longing of using television to preach the message of Christ, he pressed on. "But, God, this is an opportunity of a lifetime to reach the whole country for you!"

"Then sign the contract," God seemed to indicate to his heart.

The responsibility as well as the privilege of using television for evangelism left Paul feeling inadequate before such a mammoth task. "God, help me as I undertake this new method of communication," he prayed as he placed the contract on the desk and signed his full legal name: Paul Edwin Finkenbinder Argetsinger.

Paul thought, "I know that the evangelization of the world depends on believers in Jesus Christ. Two thousand years ago He told us, 'Go into all the world and preach the gospel to every creature,' and adds in another verse, 'I will never leave or forsake you.' Evangelism is the heart of God, but the responsibility is ours. Only God knows how many projects He has put in the hearts of his followers who have thought themselves too inadequate to accept the obligation."

"Bring 17 scripts by Thursday," the station manager directed. (This detailed information was for the camera operators to know when to make camera changes.)

Paul left the television station, his mind ecstatic with anticipation. He had no idea what a television script was, but he didn't tell the manager because he didn't want to reveal his ignorance of television. Three months later, however, station employees wondered where Paul had received his television education, because he knew more about the subject than many of them.

Paul decided that his program would be more than a televised sermon; he envisioned using Christians from our churches as actors for the portrayal of dramatized Bible stories.

The first drama featured a carpenter in his shop, sawing and nailing the boards of a cabinet. As Paul conversed with this actor-carpenter, he veered the discussion to Jesus, the master designer and carpenter of our lives. Every week the dramatized "The Church in Your Home" program ended with a brief message followed by a quartet or trio singing an appropriate hymn, and an invitation to tune in next week.

Two days after signing the television contract, Leslie Richards, a turkey grower and longtime friend from Sunnyside, Washington, surprised Paul with a knock at our door early in the morning.

Leslie had flown to Guatemala in his private plane to visit missionaries there, then decided to visit us in San Salvador. Paul invited him in. From that moment, he bombarded Leslie with the potential of television and the prospects of reaching people for Christ through that medium.

When we sat at our table for lunch, Paul noticed Leslie had placed a check beside his plate. With a lump in his throat, he saw the generous gift of $500: the largest Paul had received from any individual to that time. However, rather than seeing only a check signed by Leslie Richards, Paul envisioned the check as though God Himself had made out a blank check. In other words, Paul saw this initial gift as the beginning of Jehovah Jirah's supplying all that would be needed to fund and produce the television production.

I understood Paul's enthusiasm and endless ambition to reach the Salvadoran people for Christ. Initially I felt panicky regarding the financial commitment. Then I determined to follow the example of the biblical Gamaliel (see Acts 5:34-39)—that if Paul's undertakings were of God, He would supply the need, and if they were not of God, they were doomed to failure.

After signing the television contract, Paul was like a small child in a candy store. It was all he could talk about. It wasn't that he thought he was going to be a celebrity; rather, his only desire was to use television to propagate the gospel of Christ. With enthusiasm, brilliant eyes, and ignoring the family, his mind focused on only one thing: his radio and television programs. He seemed completely unconcerned about making the monthly payments, because he had complete confidence that God would provide.

God did supply the finances for the weekly television programs, and He did it in an assortment of ways and in an extraordinary method every month, even though we sometimes suffered the trials of our faith. On one occasion when we lacked funds, a Salvadoran woman from the country came to our home. She brought several hundred colones, the local currency, wrapped in her clothing: Exactly the amount we needed to complete that month's payment.

Early every weekday morning of the year, the task was the same. Supplied with a folding table, a thermos of coffee, my homemade cinnamon rolls, and writing pads, Paul, Raul Duron, and Phil Eldred, another missionary, went to one of the parks of the city for hours of planning the next several programs.

Life for Paul was one hectic activity after another: radio programs, rehearsals for the upcoming Sunday's drama, and compiling the material for the following Sunday. His only halfway relaxing moment with the family in the whole week was after the live Sunday evening television drama. On Monday the intense schedule began all over again.

For one entire year Paul produced a live, dramatized television program every week. One drama was the story of a potter shaping a vase then reshaping it after it had been marred by a fall, representative of Christ mending our lives when we've blemished our testimony.

"The Prodigal Son," "The Rich Man and Lazarus," "Cain and Abel," the "Healing of the Blind Man," etc., were interesting programs that depicted principles of the greatest story ever told.

The Sunday evening dramas were the topic of conversation for all El Salvador, with all eyes glued to their television sets.

Many businesses put TV sets in their display windows, and people stood in the street, intrigued with the silent performances. Many people purchased television sets, paying for them by charging their neighbors 10 or 15 centavos for watching a program; however, for "The Church in Your Home" there was no charge. A few churches drew large crowds by presenting the 7:30 p.m. television program, continuing the service immediately with joyful singing.

Juan R., a wealthy coffee plantation owner in Usulután, an eastern city of El Salvador, detested Christians. He gave evangelical employees the worst shacks and living conditions. He strictly cautioned that if anyone talked about God while working on his finca ("farm"), he or she would be fired.

Sunday nights Don Juan habitually ate his dinner and then watched television to relax. One Sunday evening he turned on the set in the middle of an exciting drama presentation, so he settled back to enjoy himself. But just as he was getting involved in the program, it was over. Then Don Juan disgustedly heard the program director announce, "And we find salvation only through Jesus Christ."

Infuriated, Juan jumped out of his chair and shut off the television. "I thought that performance was too pleasurable. Those fanatical evangelicals are tricksters." Though angry, he couldn't stop thinking about the television program. All week long Juan's intellect was haunted by the Bible drama and the penetrating words of the speaker.

The next Sunday evening, although considerably skeptical, Juan decided he would watch the entire television program. Within a couple months, Juan yielded his heart and life to Jesus Christ. He placed a television set high on a building so all his finca workers could observe the Bible dramas and learn from them. And he constructed 12 churches, the largest one on his own finca.

Fellow missionaries Arthur Lindvall and David Stewart took advantage of the popularity of the television program, visiting different towns and establishing new churches. Arthur drove tirelessly throughout the country, holding daily sessions with pastors and new leaders every weekday in one section of El Salvador after another, encouraging them and giving them literature for new converts. David, a Bible lecturer, taught the Word to new converts. Together these two men were the God-ordained spontaneous follow-up of "The Church in your Home" telecast.

Hermano Pablo, well known because of the daily radio programs and now with television, became a popular household figure in El Salvador. Paul praised God that whenever people heard his name or saw his face they associated it with God, because this had been his prayer when he began the first radio broadcast just five years earlier.

Since Paul's voice is distinctive and carries, he is recognized wherever he goes. Many times people rush up to him in restaurants while he is eating. "You must be Hermano Pablo."

A waiter in a hotel in Lima, Peru, confessed he disciplined and guided the activities of his children by what Hermano Pablo would approve.

At the end of the calendar year of 1960, the Baptists, who were in El Salvador before the Assemblies of God, sent an emissary with a letter stating: "Hermano Pablo, your program has done more to break down the prejudice against the gospel in one year than we have in the 70 years we have been in the country."

Paul's television programs were the first scheduled gospel telecasts outside the United States.

"Surely," Paul says, "it was God's timing to bring the evangelical message to the forefront as several denominations laid grueling groundwork of evangelism and had established many churches in El Salvador.

The apostle Paul said in I Corinthians 3:6: *"I planted the seed, Apollos watered it, but God made it grow."*

Paul constantly insists, "I am only a servant of Christ."

Chapter 18
Evangelizing with Movies

*The live, televised, dramatized Bible stories revealed a genuine
hunger for knowledge of God among the Salvadoran people.*

The year of live, televised, dramatized Bible stories in
1960 revealed the Salvadoran's authentic hunger for
God. The people were formerly openly antagonistic against
Protestants, but now many professionals carried on polite conversations with us, and many new people attended our evangelical churches.

El Salvador would never be the same after the live half-hour
Bible dramas thrilled as well as amazed the populace with the
previously unheard gospel of Jesus Christ. The religion of El Salvador challenged by God's Word brought amazing testimonies
from peoples of all walks of society of what the gospel of Jesus
Christ proclaimed.

In 1960 when we started television programs, the station did
not have equipment for taping the programs. Therefore, the programs were live, in black-and-white, and viewed faintly in
Nicaragua and Honduras, which brought in letters begging for
the programs in their country.

As was natural for Paul, these requests, coupled with his never-ending, adventurous ambitions, sent him on another exciting undertaking: half-hour Bible dramas on film.

Paul made a short trip to California, and God's people provided him with funds to buy a movie camera and editing equipment. While in the United States, he purchased several large rolls of black-and-white motion picture film. Jan Sadlo, a godly professional film producer from Los Angeles, returned with Paul to El Salvador to make Barrabas, the first film.

I purchased non-patterned drapery remnants and made great-looking biblical costumes. I had to shrink the material so that garments could later be laundered. I gave the material to a seamstress, describing the wide unfitted robes we needed, but when we picked up the garments, we were dismayed to see them twice the usable width. It took me all night making the drapery-material robes smaller so they'd be ready for the early Monday morning taping.

In our film of the crucifixion of Christ according to St. Matthew, Barrabas was the substitute criminal chosen when Pilate offered to free Jesus. In our Barrabas movie, we have Barrabas contemplating Jesus on the cross, and asking, "Why? Why did this innocent man have to die on the cross and not me?" Then something incredible happened at that moment—something that we couldn't have staged if we had tried. The sun went behind a cloud, symbolic of the darkness covering the earth at Christ's death almost 2,000 years earlier.

Filmmaking is completely different from live television programming. Sunlight and shadows have to be carefully calculated. We repeated scenes numerous times to eliminate speech errors, noises, and change of sunlight. After a whole day of arduous labor, only one or two minutes of actual footage could be used.

After Barrabas, Paul produced The Prodigal Son, The Calling of Matthew, and The Healing of the Leper—all drama stories complete with an ending message. The last Bible drama film produced in El Salvador was Mordecai's Noose, the story of Queen Esther. Our daughter, Bonnie, played the part of Esther.

Of course, making these films was not without weighty trials: insufficient funds, dissentions between actors, equipment breakdowns, bad weather, earthquakes, and weariness . . . just to name a few.

One morning we were up before 5 a.m., as usual. Paul was kneeling on the cold tile floor in the semi-darkness, beseeching God's help and guidance for a heavy decision facing him that day. Without warning, the earth began to violently shift and rock. A heavy wood dresser drawer flew across the room, landing on Paul's side of the bed. Had he been in the bed, he would have been severely injured. This incident is one more proof and beautiful reminiscence of how God continued to care for us.

When in 1964 we moved to the States to live, Paul, still enthralled with the potential of films, produced Elijah and Baal in color, first in Spanish and then in English.

For this film, Larry Bray, a member of the board of directors of Hermano Pablo Ministries, made a 10-foot tall statue of Baal. One Saturday we were filming a scene in the mountains in the Los Angeles area with volunteer actors from local churches.

Unexpectedly, police cars with sirens blaring rushed on to the scene and surrounded us. Police officers jumped from their vehicles demanding that we stop our activity. A neighbor had called them, reporting that drug addicts were worshipping an idol in the mountains.

Of course, we had obtained all the required permits to film in that area. Paul explained everything in his kind way and showed the police the permits. Once the mix-up was straightened out, the police officers were very understanding, asked for forgiveness, and told us to continue our filming.

One great miracle and blessing was that a professional actor, who was also a Christian, played the part of Elijah. We contracted with a man who had trained birds that we used to relate the biblical account in 1 Kings 17: ravens taking food to Elijah.

The Evangelical Film Foundation, a Christian United States organization, awarded the English version of Elijah and Baal the best Christian film of 1970.

These Bible drama films, made more than 40 years ago, feature a very young Hermano Pablo. They are now available on DVD.

Chapter 19
Paul Suffers Doubt

Having never faced faith arguments, Paul was suddenly
terrified with uncertainties and doubts, causing him
to question the authenticity of God.

"I've been preaching lies all my life," Paul declared categorically to me one Sunday evening after preaching at the Evangelistic Center. "The Bible accounts are fictitious; the Israelites couldn't have crossed the Red Sea on dry ground, Daniel couldn't have remained alive all night in a lions den," Paul proclaimed scornfully. "Furthermore, it's impossible for men to walk in a fiery furnace and live to tell about it."

With uncontrollable tears streaming down my face, I slumped weakly in my chair, aghast at what my minister-husband was saying. We had shared the gospel for 20 years; I could not believe what I was hearing.

That evening several people had turned the kingship of their lives to God after the gospel message Paul had delivered. He remembers how after preaching the evening message, as he sat down, his intellect screamed at him. "You liar! You know the Bible isn't true!"

The six-year airing of the daily radio programs on YSU plus the weekly programs for a year on television had touched the hearts of the Salvadoran people to believe in Christ. Now it was Paul himself who doubted God; this left me fearful and horrified. Alarmed at the change in Paul—and nervous about God's retribution—I objected to Paul's distorted logic. But nothing I said dissuaded him. In fact, when he heard me pray, he scolded me. "Prayer is a sham because there is no God!"

I continued to pray for him that the Holy Spirit of God would show him the truth.

Three months prior to this, Paul, another minister of the gospel, and I were returning to San Salvador from Santa Ana. Without warning, we came upon road repairs, with one lane of the two-lane highway blocked off. Racing toward us in our lane was a large construction truck. Paul swerved the car to the right, but the truck hit the left front of our car, spinning it around like a top. This near-death accident caused considerable car damage, but God had miraculously protected us from injury.

Paul's friend, Neco Mac Entee, heard of the accident and rushed to our rescue and took us to a hotel. Once we were settled in, he asked, "What happened?"

Pablo, ever mindful of God's sovereignty and using the opportunity to explain this to Neco, told him, "Satan wanted to kill me up ahead, but God stopped me here."

With this experience so recent in our minds, how could Paul no longer believe in the sovereignty of God?

Paul recalls, "Those doubts and fears left me feeling empty inside. I couldn't pray. But I still had to make my daily radio programs and fulfill other responsibilities, even though I felt they were in vain."

During this horrible battle of distrust in God, who, heretofore, had always been Paul's confidence and peace, Paul received a letter from Carolyn Lindblad, a Zion Bible School classmate. It was the first time she had written him. Carolyn's timely, caring letter was just what he needed. She wrote:

"Paul, I've had a haunting nightmare about you that isn't the Paul I know, and I'm deeply upset and concerned for you. In the dream, you were dressed in the most deplorable dirty-rags condition, like a common street beggar, and when I asked you if you didn't have anything better to wear, you said you were like that all over. The dream has distressed me, Paul, and I've spent two weeks obtaining your address because God wants me to tell you that you are on God's heart and He loves you very much."

I never imagined that Paul would tell Carolyn about his doubts and fears. He responded immediately, confessing his deplorable faith problem, the ragged clothes, symbolic of his spiritual condition. "I'm like that all over, Carolyn. Please continue to pray for me."

Carolyn's words greatly encouraged Paul, although doubts and fears continued to overwhelm him. Meditating constantly, Paul remembered seeing illiterate people in Guatemala climbing mountain trails to worship stick or stone gods, taking fruit, flowers, and food to their fabricated god. Paul eventually concluded that God created man with a spiritual nature. Worship is a normal component of human behavior, and God made man with faith.

Deliberation of these thoughts and reading the Bible continually out of the necessity to produce his radio programs brought renewed faith to his heart. His restored confidence in God, which included the Bible miracles, awarded Paul the joy and happiness he had previously known.

It was Paul's reading of self-help books declaring that the miracles in men's lives are self-created that caused this frightening incident in his life. Regretfully and shamefully Paul neglected evaluating and comparing this reading material with God's Word, which had served Him so many years. He says, "I know this was an attack of Satan himself against me, my testimony, and my message. The phenomenal success of my daily evangelical radio program for six years, plus the whole year of 1960 with live television, had changed the mentality of the Salvadoran people. Satan wasn't successful in taking my life in the car accident, and I praise God that he didn't succeed in destroying my faith."

Paul's frightening loss of faith experience educated him, enhanced his understanding of faith, and equipped him more adequately to assist questioning hearts that come to him for help.

"Today my severely tested faith experience in a holy, divine God is unwavering," Paul proclaims. "Losing faith in God has been the most terrifying experience of my life."

Chapter 20
Communicating Pentecostalism

Hermano Pablo was accepted by all evangelical denominations, and was probably the one person everyone would listen to regarding an explanation of the Holy Spirit experience.

A sometimes "hot" topic of conversation among Christians in both Latin and North America at this time was the question of the baptism of the Spirit, particularly speaking in tongues. Paul was asked to speak to a gathering of interdenominational leaders on this subject. The following is his letter regarding his dissertation on Pentecost as he reported it to his father, Rev. Frank Finkenbinder, after attending a conference in Costa Rica.

Sept. 2, 1963
Dear Dad,

I have just returned from one of the most fabulous experiences of my life. The 70-year-old Latin American Mission in Costa Rica, made up of several denominations, mostly non-Pentecostal, invited me to a conference for leaders on Evangelism and Communication.

The first week was the leadership seminar on Evangelism, and I had a two-hour class Tuesday through Fri-

113

day to present talks on communication. This was my first time to present this class on communication, which does not represent any particular aspect of evangelism. Rather, it is an explanation of a way to communicate the gospel.

Since taking the Dale Carnegie Leadership Training Course, I've read several books on this subject and found it an interesting field although neglected by most people. I felt a bit nervous facing this diverse audience, filling my time with various skits and illustrations and opening the last hour for discussion and questions.

In one skit, with a volunteer standing below and facing forward in front of me, I stood on a chair holding my coat, which represents the gospel of Jesus Christ. I explained in my skit that I am a rank sinner and know nothing of the gospel (the coat), and the volunteer's task (a Christian attempting to evangelize) is to tell me how to put the coat on without looking at me.

The volunteer is facing forward and cannot see me because the Christian cannot know or see the heart or thoughts of a person he is witnessing to.

The volunteer tells me to pick up the coat by the collar. For this illustration, I do not know what the collar is, so I pick the coat up by the bottom or side. Without seeing me, he asks if I see two long tubes. I agree there are two dangling parts. He asks me to put my arms into them, which I do by putting my hand in the bottom of one sleeve and then the other, after which he tells me to put it around me. Of course, my coat is a tangled up mess and the congregation is laughing.

Finally, the volunteer turns to see what I have done. In essence, this demonstration illustrates that our Christian jargon does not always speak the language of the person we are evangelizing because they do not understand our Christian language.

Many times our words do not communicate because we have not established a friendship with that person. Our lives have to be an example and our words must be in terms they can understand.

Dr. Kenneth Stracken, Director of the Latin American Mission, had made a trip to El Salvador to invite me to speak to their conference on Pentecost. I gave him an emphatic "no", even though I strongly sensed that he personally wanted to know about the subject. One thing I want to mention is that Dr. Stracken is the godliest person I have been near who actually radiated the presence of Christ.

The first week of the conference, Dr. Stracken insisted that I speak on the doctrine of Pentecost. He wanted my point of view regarding the baptism of the Holy Spirit, particularly in speaking in tongues, and reserved two hours on Thursday of the second week.

I protested, saying I did not want to break the harmony of this multi-denominational group but finally conceded at his insistence as others were requesting that I speak.

You can imagine, Dad, the tremendous challenge this was. Here were gathered all these denominations representing all the counties of Latin America, and probably most of them had prejudices against the Pentecostal experience. I was thrust into the task of presenting the message of Pentecost in a way they could understand and, what's more, accept.

Fortunately, the day before I was to present my talk

on Pentecost, almost as if by chance, I was invited for lunch to the home of Presbyterian Kenneth and Elizabeth Hood. Mr. Hood was a Professor of Systematic Theology in Costa Rica. Would you believe we sat at the table from 12:15 until 5:15 without moving, talking about the work of the Holy Spirit? They wanted to know what I was going to present the next day, and I asked them to ask questions, which helped me understand their problems. This was exactly the experience I needed to help me present the matter of Pentecost to such a varied group of denominations, personalities, and races.

I had a dinner engagement in another home, but this couple insisted I return in the evening, and from 7 p.m. till midnight, a total of nine hours that day, we talked about my next day's theme.

I spoke about Pentecost for an hour and a half, opening with a sincere admission of guilt and asking forgiveness for Pentecostals who place more importance on tongues than on love, some even arrogantly claiming they might not have a great education but they have the power of the Holy Spirit.

Using a blackboard, I drew a circle representing God. Under God, I drew a line representing our minds, and under the line I drew another circle representing man. I explained God guides us through our intellect, speaking to us through our minds, be it in writing, a vision, or His promptings; and man communicates with God through verbal language.

At times, with the pressures of life—illnesses, tragedies, disaster, or calamities—we cry out to God in our spirits. Many times we cry out in anguish, without words as the Scripture states in Romans 8:23, *"Even we ourselves groan within ourselves."* I told them that I call speaking in tongues breaking the barrier of the mind, establishing a direct communication with God, for only He knows the anguish of our souls or the euphoria and joy of His blessings that flow over us. The baptism of the Holy Spirit is an infilling of love and of power, manifesting greater faith and confidence in God's promises.

Another valuable dimension regarding speaking in tongues is that Satan cannot interfere with our prayers, since he cannot understand the spirit language. *"Likewise the Spirit also helps our infirmities: for we know not what we should pray for as we ought; but the spirit itself makes intercession for the saints with groanings which cannot be uttered. And he that searches the hearts knows what is in the mind of the Spirit, because he makes intercession for the saints according to the will of God"* (Rom. 8:26-27).

I stressed that Pentecost is not a denomination but rather an experience, and receiving the baptism of the Holy Spirit did not mean changing a denomination but simply experiencing closeness to God. Nevertheless, many people who have not received this experience live closer to God than some people once filled with God's spirit and no longer living dedicated to Him.

When I finished my presentation, there were three dissenting comments, one being, "We have heard this man's opinion and I think we should dismiss the service immediately." I willingly agreed to step aside, but a man jumped to his feet, saying that he needed the experience, so the meeting continued with another man quoting one Scripture after another, which I was explaining, but when he continued with many questions, the group told him he was monopolizing the time and others wanted to speak.

A brother from Venezuela said in his younger days while he was studying the Bible with his brother, the spirit of God came over them and they both spoke in tongues, but they did not understand the experience and never told anyone about it. A Plymouth Brethren man said he felt like he was lacking something in his life, but now he knew what it is. Another leader thanked those responsible for having me speak on the matter of Pentecost, because this is what the church of Christ needs.

Someone asked if speaking in tongues was the definite evidence of the baptism of the Holy Spirit. I told him the best way I could answer his question was by saying that speaking in tongues represents a complete submission of the mind and will to God's Holy Spirit.

God helped me in this biggest challenge I have had thus far, without losing friendship with these people, while presenting the baptism of the Holy Spirit in a constructive, helpful way. There were many words of gratitude for my speaking, and I received several invitations to speak to leaders of other denominations.

I know you and Mom will appreciate this testimony of what I am doing.

Your son,
Paul

Paul's emphasis on the Pentecostal experience is that it isn't a religion but an experience.

Years later several of these leaders reported that the Pentecostal experience is now real in their lives.

Chapter 21
Our Marriage is Tested

*Divorce was never an option for Paul and me. It certainly
would have destroyed Paul's ministry because Satan takes
advantage of any negligence and tries to destroy a marriage
or life any way he can.*

In 1964 we felt we had completed our mission in El Salvador and decided to return to the United States to live with
our children. Paul and Gene were attending universities in California.

Though not on the mission field, Paul continued Hermano
Pablo Ministries. In fact, he was busier than ever, so busy that
he forgot to include me in his activities. Over a period of time,
he began to neglect me.

Paul believed our unhappy marriage was normal; he blamed
me for our unhappiness. I worked as a secretary at Hermano
Pablo Ministries when Paul began criticizing everything I said
or did. He demonstrated embarrassment of me. His outstanding
personality changed completely, seemingly making him another
person; I felt embarrassed by his actions as a minister of the
gospel of Jesus Christ.

I did everything possible to keep anyone from knowing that
the famous Hermano Pablo was no longer the sweet, charming

man who had swept me off my feet 35 years earlier. I did not tell anyone about our unhappy life. Brokenhearted and grief-stricken, my entreaties to God were my only comfort, especially in the middle of the night when the man sleeping by my side was no longer mine.

Every four-minute "A Message to the Conscience" radio program heard throughout Central and South America took Paul at least two hours to prepare. Then Paul added a daily 15-minute English radio broadcast to his already-busy schedule, which included a succession of crusades in Latin America.

Paul felt obligated to accept every invitation made to him. Keeping current with the two daily radio programs and the many crusades became a very difficult work schedule. The action-packed days did not contain enough hours to accomplish the daily demands, although Paul worked until midnight daily writing and recording radio programs. Little by little, in his rare moments of relaxation, Paul began to fellowship more with his singer, Manuel, and colleague minister, Hector, than with me.

I could no longer accept Paul's inattention. He had stopped demonstrating tenderness and kindness. Even though in my heart I knew that he loved me, I decided running away from home would possibly attract Paul's attention. Even though he no longer treated me as his companion, I knew he would disregard his numerous responsibilities, call the police, and search the California highways until he found me.

The very week I anticipated running away, I fell on a step in a restaurant, breaking my left ankle. I ended up in the hospital, desiring that my neck instead of my ankle had been broken. If Paul didn't love me, I had nothing to live for.

Looking back one can recognize errors. Paul and I believe that the excess work is what led to the negligence of reading God's Word and undoubtedly daily consecration. Satan continuously scrutinizes our unguarded spiritual weak spots as an opportunity to destroy our relationships with God. In our case, he determined to destroy our marriage.

After four or five years of this kind of conflict, Paul recognized that we could not continue to ignore the unhappiness in our home. Therefore, in 1979 he called a marriage counselor friend, Rev. Mel Johnson, from Southern California College, now Vanguard University, for counsel. Mr. Johnson came to our home and over dinner listened patiently to our resentments. It hurt to hear Paul criticize me as well as my manner of speaking, because these were totally opposite of the warm Hispanic way of communicating. I explained briefly to Mr. Johnson that Paul disapproved of me and criticized everything I did.

Mr. Johnson listened attentively to both our comments, and almost instantly directed solemn words to Paul that changed our lives completely. "Paul, you treat better and pay more attention to your ministry companions coming in and out of your life than you do Linda, your best friend, who will be by your side until you die. Your responsibility is to be considerate of her, protecting, defending, paying attention to her, and accepting her opinions above others."

Miraculously, Paul recognized his failings and changed his attitude from one moment to the next. Paul changed from a stern, inflexible, macho husband to an affectionate, compassionate husband. He honored me with expressions of respect and appreciation. The change in Paul was so astonishing and radical I had difficulty believing and accepting it; I questioned if I could trust it to be genuine and lasting.

I forgave Paul verbally, but his past actions had caused such great wounds that I couldn't forget them. Without forgetting, I knew that my forgiveness was not complete. I continued to cry and pray in the middle of the night, except now my bitter tears were not against Paul but because of the pain in my heart. He had hurt me so much that I felt resentful. Years later I recognized that my resentment was a sin before God—just as Paul's mistreatment of me had been.

Paul believed after repenting and his change of attitude that all of the past should be forgotten. He couldn't understand how his words and actions had offended and damaged my confidence in myself. His "I'm sorry; forgive me" didn't heal my heart.

Some three months after Paul's dramatic change in character, I awoke in the night, remembering the wounds Paul had caused. Satan was telling me that Paul didn't know the pain he had caused, and he didn't deserve forgiveness.

I arose from bed and in the darkness of our living room, fell to my knees, and cried for hours, until I had no more tears. When I finally became quiet before God, I sensed His Holy presence like a peaceful cloud filling the entire room and a gentle voice saying, "Linda, ask for what you want."

Feeling totally unworthy and undeserving before the awesome presence of God, I cried out, "Powerful God, please give me a sufficient amount of your power to forgive and forget all this hurt."

Instantly I was liberated. God removed the bitterness in my heart, healed my mixed emotions, and granted me complete victory over the past. I never thought it possible to experience anything so dramatic and powerful.

I felt an unbelievable peace. Without forgiving Paul, it would have been impossible to have a peaceful matrimony. Besides, forgiving Paul is the greatest gift I could ever bestow on myself.

Satan tried many times to make me remember the past and condemn Paul again for his past action instead of leaving them buried as Christ has buried our sins.

We reinstated daily family altar that we had neglected during the busy years. Besides our individual Bible reading, at the breakfast table every morning Paul reads a Proverb or Psalm, and I pray; the next day I read the Bible and Paul leads in prayer. It is impossible to emphasize the value and importance of reading the Bible and praying together every day.

Reading the Bible and praying together brought healing and happiness to our lives. Our marriage now is like a continual honeymoon, with a profound love that we never believed possible.

At the same time, reading the Bible and praying together make arguments difficult.

Only God could perform the miracle in our hearts—both Paul's and mine. Our marriage, as well as Paul's ministry in the Hispanic world, was rescued by the power of God, who changed Paul's attitude and helped me forgive my life companion.

Chapter 22

One Hundred Free Radio Stations

The radio ministry of Hermano Pablo continued to increase.

From our home in California, Paul continued without interruption his "A Message to the Conscience" radio programs. He built a tiny six-foot-square recording studio in a corner of the garage of the home we purchased in Costa Mesa.

Paul recorded his radio programs in his miniscule radio studio. A secretary worked at our dining room table in the house. One day Paul told me an employee needed to use a desk in one of our daughter's bedroom.

Immediately I protested. "We must find an office for our ministry."

Paul asked me to remain patient, that our limited budget was not sufficient to rent an office.

"God, in His Word, promises to provide our needs, and an office for this ministry is a genuine need," I declared emphatically.

In spite of Paul's objection, I drove the Costa Mesa streets until I found precisely what we needed: an upstairs complex of four rooms in a building where Jean Music, the owner, kept electronic instruments. He wanted $300 a month rent. I insisted that Paul go to see it.

Two secretaries accompanied Paul and me to the building. We climbed the stairs to the second floor, and without a word, Paul inspected the perfect-for-us office space. As we were exiting the room, Paul raised his arm to heaven. "Lord, I claim this whole building for you in Jesus' name!"

With renewed faith, Paul enthusiastically envisioned the first floor warehouse of the building for the future television studio of his dreams. He then moved the offices out of our home and into the second-floor rooms of the building on Placentia Avenue.

The radio ministry continually expanded. One day our six-foot-four, distinguished-looking son-in-law Jonathan Brown went to the post office in Costa Mesa, explained Hermano Pablo's ministry to the clerk, and told him that Hispanics needed an easy-to-remember post office box number. He came home with P. O. Box 100.

On another day in 1967, quite out of the blue, Jonathan presented Paul with a proposal. "Dad, how would you like to have your four-minute radio programs on 100 radio stations?"

Paul patted Jon on the back. "Jon, you are playing with my most sensitive emotions when you speak of blanketing the Spanish world with our radio program. Where would I possibly get finances for 100 radio stations? I have difficulty paying for the 26 we have now."

"Don't let money alarm you, Dad. I'm offering the radio stations the "A Message to the Conscience" program in exchange for gratis air time."

"That is preposterous. Who ever heard of free radio time?" Paul believed Jon's plan was impossible.

"We'll never know if we don't offer this once-in-a-lifetime opportunity to the radio stations to air an invaluable program that will bless their people," Jon argued. "I'll write to the radio stations informing them that "A Message to the Conscience" program never speaks of political issues and is spiritual and moral but not religious. We never ask for money, and it lifts the morale of the listener. The only thing they have to do is say they want it."

"Jon, the radio station managers will be distrustful of your proposal and will recognize that you're asking for gratuitous air time."

"How can anybody be distrustful of such a precious message? If they will just listen to the program, they will realize the value it is for their radio listeners."

Jon continued to argue for his idea. His undaunted enthusiasm was contagious. It wasn't too long before Paul began to reflect on our son-in-law's plan.

"Dad, I've already written to the mayors of the prominent cities of Latin America, asking them for the names of their most popular radio stations and their current managers. I have the handbook of all the Spanish radio stations in Latin America. I will write to all these stations and they will respond if they want it."

Paul didn't want to put a restraint on Jon's youthful enthusiasm, although he still doubted that Jon's plan was realistic. But it was worth the try, so he gave his approval.

Jon's mother, Thelma (now with the Lord) laboriously typed envelopes with the names and addresses of the 3,300 media stations from the Handbook of Latin American Radio Stations. She had no knowledge of Spanish, so she carefully checked the spelling of the Hispanic names and addresses one letter at a time. Meanwhile, Jon wrote a straightforward letter explaining his project and translated it into Spanish. Since it was before the age of computers, he mimeographed a copy for all 3,300 stations.

Within a month, "A Message to the Conscience" program was on a little more than 100 radio stations and all free of charge.

Paul's problem was to continue paying on the 26 stations. God in His sovereignty knew a future financial dilemma could possibly end the radio ministry, and Jon's implementation of his offer to radio stations saved Hermano Pablo Ministries from extinction.

"I admire the great faith, determination, and dedication of my son-in-law," Paul always affirms.

One interesting report of how the "A Message to the Conscience" broadcast has resulted in blessing the radio stations came to us from the state of Rhode Island. A radio listener in Ecuador moved to the United States and took a cassette of 12 "A Message to the Conscience" programs to a local radio station for them to broadcast.

The management had absolutely no interest in the program, but the man from Ecuador was so persistent for many weeks that the station manager decided to air the programs. When the 12 days of programs had been broadcast, the manager thought that was the end of the "problem." What he hadn't expected was the multitude of telephone calls to the station asking for more programs. In desperation, the manager called our offices in Costa Mesa, asking us to send him programs immediately.

The "A Message to the Conscience" program augments the listener audience to a radio station.

Chapter 23
The First Crusade for the Masses

After moving to California in 1964, Paul began to receive invitations to hold evangelism crusades in different countries.

In 1966, one important invitation for Paul to hold Assemblies of God evangelistic crusades came from the missionaries in Bolivia, a country with three distinct living areas: La Paz, Santa Cruz, and Cochabamba.

The prospects of crusades in Bolivia interested Paul, because it was the country to which he first felt God had called him for evangelism; however, he felt strongly that the crusades should not be just for the Assemblies of God. His radio audience included all denominations, and this crusade would affect all future crusades.

Paul wrote the crusade leader of his misgivings. This man insisted that Paul owed it to our shared denomination—as they paid for the radio time in Bolivia. Through a series of back-and-forth letters, the crusade leader disputed Paul's loyalty to the denomination.

In the end Paul reluctantly relented and accepted going to Bolivia for the Assemblies of God crusades. He wrote the crusade leader of his decision; however, the instant he dropped the letter to Bolivia in the post office, he knew he had erred and felt sick because he belonged to the whole body of Christ, not just a denomination. His message was for everyone, and Paul didn't want to draw people from other denominations to his. His desire was to unite the body of Christ, permitting individuals to accept Christ and attend the evangelical churches of their choice.

That same year Paul received an invitation to participate in Billy Graham's first conference on evangelism. While in Berlin, Germany, he met Bruno Frigoli, an Assemblies of God Bolivian missionary, who knew nothing of the correspondence between Paul and the other missionary.

Bruno was a former bodyguard of Mussolini. A tough, dynamic, strong-willed individual, he fled to Bolivia when the Italian dictator lost his position. After many years in Bolivia, missionary Everett Hale picked up a hitchhiking Bruno one day and invited him to an evangelical service. In appreciation for the ride, Bruno accepted Hale's invitation and through this contact, he found Christ as His Savior and became a minister of the gospel of Jesus Christ.

Paul explained his dilemma of not wanting his first crusade only to be for one denomination. Bruno, with his usual dynamism, said, "Don't worry, Pablo. I'll fix it and we'll open up the services to everyone."

That was his offer and he arranged it.

In May and June of 1967, Paul spent two weeks each in Cochabamba, Santa Cruz, and La Paz, Bolivia, where the city altitude of 11,000 feet, required his using oxygen while speaking.

The city of La Paz, the highest capital in the world, set in a basin 3,000 feet below the high mountain ridge of 14,000 feet, gave Paul a beautiful welcome. They placed many dozens of metal 55-gallon barrels filled with oily rags around the mountain edge, forming the words Bienvenido Hermano Pablo, "Welcome Brother Paul." The oily rags burned brilliantly all night, lighting up the whole countryside the first night of the La Paz crusade, announcing Hermano Pablo's presence in the city. Sadly, no one thought to take a picture of the extraordinary scene.

The six weeks Paul spent in Bolivia were the longest and most difficult times of separation he and I have endured. We wrote letters to each other daily, even though the letters took eight days to arrive.

The following is Paul's condensed account of the Cochabamba and Aruba Crusades.

"Oh, what a fantastic service we enjoyed tonight in a small coliseum with 3,000 in attendance. I had prayed that at least 100 people would surrender their hearts and lives to Christ, and at least 200 people prayed the Sinner's Prayer of repentance. God has manifested His divine blessing in every service, as some 700 people reportedly have given the Lordship of their lives to God in this 12-day meeting.

"In addition, another 120 people accepted the Lord in one service in Oruro, where we flew in a small 185 Cessna plane that almost didn't make it over the 16,500-foot mountain."

Missionary Monroe Grams also reported on the La Paz Crusade. "'A Message to the Conscience' radio program has been heard in Bolivia since 1959. Enter any home, office, or taxi and mention Hermano Pablo, and almost everyone knows him. Even Catholic priests and nuns listen to his program. The Holy Spirit has used Paul to bring the knowledge of Christ to many people. Every night after a moving message, he gives an opportunity to accept Christ. While the choir is singing, "Come to Jesus," Paul folds his arms and waits. The people respond from all areas of the amphitheater. Some nights 500 people came to the altar to ask for forgiveness of their sins. In total, there are 2,500 cards of conversions."

Paul's last letters from Bolivia gave this account: "The last 12-day campaign in the jungle area of Santa Cruz drew the same interest as in La Paz and Cochabamba. The coliseum seated only 2,500 people. One thousand more chairs were brought in for the crowds, and on the last night, hundreds were left standing. The interesting thing is that it rained hard practically every day, usually just before the service. Twice it rained during the service. I became completely drenched to the skin, and the people stayed in their seats listening to my message. Nine hundred twenty sin-burdened people openly acknowledged Jesus Christ as their Lord and Savior in these last two weeks of services in Santa Cruz."

Well over 4,000 people came to know Jesus in the six-week crusades in Bolivia, with a total attendance of 50,000 people. In La Paz and in Santa Cruz, local radio stations broadcast the crusade services every evening for all of Bolivia to hear. The local radio stations of the three cities he visited in Bolivia invited Paul for interviews, bringing Hermano Pablo's voice with the message of Christ to all of Bolivia.

A reporter, admiring Paul's enthusiasm, asked him if he had ever considered selling commercials. Paul flashed him a big smile. "No, I doubt that I could sell a tube of toothpaste, or anything that does not offer eternal life, with enthusiasm."

Because he suffered with constant pain, pure determination and optimism kept Paul going in Bolivia. When Paul left Los Angeles with his singer, Manuel Bonilla, on that evening plane flight for Bolivia, he looked like a gaunt, tired old man because of a very large duodenal ulcer. Paul and I had celebrated our 25th wedding anniversary at home on January 25 with Paul's diet of Cream of Wheat and ginger ale with cream.

In the homes that hosted him, Paul politely ate whatever food was set before him, even when he knew it was injurious to his stomach.

When I said good-bye to Paul at the airport, I seriously believed I might not see him alive again, but I knew he would be happy to die evangelizing in Bolivia. Deeply concerned regarding Paul's suffering, according to his letters, I attended Faith Center, Rev. Ray Schlock's church in Glendale, California, to ask prayer for Paul's healing.

After a month of misery in Bolivia, Paul's pain amazingly and suddenly vanished, and he enjoyed food and strong coffee without pain.

As I continued to pray for him, I sensed a deep, inner peace for Paul, but I didn't learn of his betterment until he stepped off the plane in Los Angeles. I was amazed, as he appeared 10 years younger.

A few weeks later, I kept an appointment with my physician, Dr. Fisher, who inquired about Paul. He was mystified because Paul had not been in to see him. Paul had written him from Bolivia, saying he wanted surgery right away because he had too much to do to put up with his painful ulcer. I explained that Paul had come home from Bolivia without a sign of the ulcer pain.

Dr. Fisher responded, "That sounds good, but I can't believe it without making tests."

Paul submitted to the tests for Dr. Fisher. Two days later an astonished doctor called with the test results. "Paul, I don't understand this. I have your former X-ray before me, where you have a golf ball-size ulcer. But this new X-ray shows that your stomach is like that of a new baby."

Paul responded, "God blessed my Bolivia crusades, and He healed me of a menacing golf ball-size ulcer as an extra bonus!"

Chapter 24
The Hardest Decision

In order to obey his convictions, Paul felt obligated to break fellowship with our Assemblies of God denomination.

"How do you know it's God's will for you to be His voice to the Hispanic world?" A denominational leader, skeptical of Paul's ambitious radio dreams, inquired.

"I never thought of it that way," Paul responded respectfully. "I think of it as my contribution to the kingdom of God and I don't think God will refuse me. I know it sounds ostentatious, but my desire is that every Hispanic person of the world will think of God when he or she hears my voice."

Paul found it difficult explaining his heart's desire to the denominational leaders who met with him in Long Beach, California, in 1968. They offered to pull out all stops, eliminating all concern for finances if Paul would hold crusades only for our own denomination.

Paul didn't want to be insensitive or discourteous to their feelings, but his heart dictated he should minister to the whole body of Christ in the Spanish world. "No amount of money can make me be unfaithful to my calling."

Three years after renting the office space from Mr. Music, the owner announced he was selling the building. He offered it to us for $95,000. He wanted $25,000 down, and he would carry the loan for us so we would not need to go through a bank. This was an unanticipated miracle because with our low income, we could never have qualified for a bank loan.

Paul thanked Mr. Music for giving him the first option to buy and left his office jubilant with the fantasy dream of owning the whole building—never mind that he didn't have a nickel for the purchase!

Two weeks later, a generous donor friend in Kenosha, Wisconsin, Walter Block, passed away. Paul attended his funeral. During the memorial service, Hattie, Walter's widow, said her husband anticipated leaving a contribution for our ministry. She asked, "Paul, what do you need?"

He reminded her that they were at Walter's funeral and shouldn't be speaking of his needs.

She responded that he was not in Chicago often, and she needed to speak to him then.

Finally, Paul said, "Hattie, I need a radio recording studio."

"Where would you put the recording studio?" Hattie inquired with curiosity.

"I'd rent another room in the office building I'm in now."

Hattie shook her head. "I don't want to invest money in anything rented. What would the building cost?"

Paul was stunned, because the building had come up for sale just two weeks before. When Paul gave Hattie the figures she immediately said, "I'll give you $25,000. Here's $4,000 to hold the building, and I'll send the balance when probate closes."

Proudly, contemplating the thought of the ministry owning its own building, Paul left the funeral reception feeling 10-feet tall and walking on air.

Paul confirmed the purchase of the building with the $4,000. When the $21,000 arrived from Hattie Block for the down payment of the building, Paul's ministry board discussed under what name to buy the building. They had three options: (1) The General Council of the Assemblies of God; (2) one of the local board member's churches; or (3) incorporate the ministry with its own name. The board's decision was to incorporate the ministry, later duly recorded in the State of California as Hermano Pablo Ministries, Inc.

The minutes of this decision went to our denominational headquarters. Within two weeks a letter informed Paul that if he incorporated, he would jeopardize his credentials with our denomination because the denominational laws at that time prohibited personal ministry incorporations.

The possibility of losing his credentials with the Assemblies of God brought him great anxiety. In anguish he took the letter, his Bible, and a yellow writing pad and sequestered himself in a local motel for three days to seek God's guidance. He wrote his thoughts: the pros and cons of this important decision, evaluating the cost of severing fellowship with our denomination. Pained and sad, Paul realized he had to give up his ministry credentials, but he deliberated many days before actually carrying it out.

Paul spent sleepless nights closer to depression than I have ever seen him. He walked about grim faced, anguished, crying often, brokenhearted with the contemplation of severing association with the Assemblies of God, which he had belonged to all his life.

One night in a vivid dream Paul observed a graphic image of his predicament as well as the dreadful solution. In his dream, he saw himself flying short distances in an airplane, which represented (for him) the Assemblies of God. The plane crashed a couple times (previous conflicts) with minor damages. Then the plane crashed and was damaged beyond repair. Paul saw himself exiting the plane and walking alone slowly and forlornly into the future in front of the plane.

This dream portraying a break with his denomination brought even more anguish of spirit. One day Paul seemed more distraught than usual. Our son Paul suggested we attend a morning prayer service that our friend, the Rev. Ralph Wilkerson, held each Thursday at Melodyland near the entrance to Disneyland in Anaheim, California.

At the family's insistence, Paul agreed. While there, he filled in a prayer request paper indicating he needed prayer and signed his name. At the end of the service an elder of Melodyland asked if he wanted special prayer right then or just wanted his name on the prayer list.

Our son and I insisted on special prayer right then for the completely dejected Hermano Pablo. The elder returned, saying that Pastor Wilkerson, who knew Paul personally, wanted to see him in his private office.

When Ralph came into his office and saw Paul slumped in a chair, before greeting him, he dismissed everyone from the room except Paul and me. With great sympathy and compassion, he looked at Paul. Led powerfully by the Holy Spirit of God, he said, "I don't have the slightest idea what your difficulty is, but whatever your uncertainty is, it isn't of God because God is not a God of confusion."

Ralph's words confirmed in Paul's mind the unavoidable break with the Assemblies of God. So in 1972 with bleeding heart and vacillating thoughts, Paul wrote three irrevocable letters of resignation and sent one to the General Council, another to the Foreign Missions Board, and the third to the Southern California District of the Assemblies of God.

Paul's resignation needed the denomination's approval in case he had broken some moral rule. In addition, they said all of his office and radio equipment belonged to the denomination. Without bitterness or resentment, willing to put his typewriter on any old desk, Paul responded immediately. "Advise me, brethren, of your instructions, or back up a truck and take all the office and movie equipment."

Three weeks later the denomination wrote again saying they appreciated Paul's spirit and were going to give him everything except the Speed the Light movie equipment he had bought. Rev. Ralph Wilkerson of Melodyland intervened and kindly picked up this depreciation-prorated tab of $6,000 for him.

"My resignation from the Assemblies of God," Paul says, "and relinquishing my credentials with them is the most difficult and painful decision I have ever made. God knows I harbor no resentment against the Assemblies of God or against their policies. I realize that at that time, there just wasn't a department for my interdenominational evangelistic ministry."

Immediately we lost our income and our 27-year radio ministry lost all financial support. Even though Paul's "Message to the Conscience" radio program was now on 100 radio stations free of charge, he owed payments on 26. Paul wrote the 26 stations, advising them that because of a critical financial crisis, he could no longer pay to remain on their stations. However, he advised, he would be happy to send them the radio programs if they would like to continue airing them on their station. Only one station declined. Mercifully, God had intervened for the radio ministry, which could have ended drastically if Jonathan, our son-in-law, had not secured free radio-station time four years before this.

Fifteen years later, in 1987, after two renowned ministers shocked the world with their scandalous immoral testimonies and leaving many disillusioned believers, Paul was holding a crusade in Temuco, Chile.

A dozen media journalists attended the press conference scheduled the first afternoon. The reporters began with all the usual questions regarding his name, purpose for being in Temuco, etc., after which they brought up the scandals that greatly affected Latin America. Their clear inference and unmistakably sarcasm was that Hermano Pablo also entertained that same kind of lifestyle. Paul patiently attempted to evade the persistent abusive questions associating him with those other ministers.

In press conferences, or any other situation, Paul maintains his composure, but the mockery of these reporters annoyed him deeply. He evaded the outlandish questions for several minutes. Finally, he jumped to his feet and unable to keep his irritability from his voice he fired some questions at the reporters. "How is it that if a movie star has an outlandish moral affair, it doesn't make news? Or why isn't it news when your president or you or anyone has a shocking love affair?" Becoming animated, he continued. "I'll tell you why. It's because a moral stain isn't noticeable on an impure life, because dirt on dirt isn't visible. Do you want to know why it is an enormous international scandal if a minister of the gospel of Jesus Christ has a moral failure? It's because a moral blemish on the pure, unadulterated gospel of Jesus Christ shows up conspicuously before the whole world."

With Paul's emotional outburst, the press conference ended abruptly without further comments.

The fall of these highly visible ministers of the gospel got Paul to thinking about accountability—someone to whom he should be responsible. He'd been out from the covering of the Assemblies of God for 15 years. During that time, the denomination's leaders to whom Paul had sent his resignation had been replaced with new leaders. These men had been asking Paul to reinstate his credentials. So in 1987 Paul once again received the credentials of the Assemblies of God.

Chapter 25
Paul Averts a Suicide

*God used Paul to present the message of salvation
to a man who was attempting suicide.*

D r. Alfredo Ortiz Mancia, Minister of Salvadoran Foreign
Affairs of El Salvador, who invited us to his home for
dinner, interrupted the conversation. "Hermano Pablo, my butler
informs me that a messenger at the door says he came to take you
to a distraught man who is determined to commit suicide tonight;
however, this man has agreed to speak with you if you will go to
him."

Seated in the place of honor at a very large table adorned with
flowers and candles, Paul had just given thanks to God for the
food when the butler entered the room.

Immediately, Paul courteously excused himself from our dinner host, accompanied the messenger to the Carlos Valiente
home, where a half-crazed man threatened to take his life.

We were well acquainted with the Valiente family, owners of
a prestigious gold and silver ornament store. In 1960 all of the
family had come to Christ as a result of the television programs.
Some time later, they rented a hall, calling it Josue Auditorium
and held Sunday morning services to share the gospel of Jesus
Christ with their friends. Years later, in 1984, this group joined

with our Friday night group to become the prestigious Josue Church.

Paul arrived at the Valiente home. Ignoring the revolver that the agitated man brandished menacingly, Paul thanked the man, named Arturo, for agreeing to speak with him. In a gentle compassionate voice, Paul spoke to the man. "What's wrong, Arturo? Why do you want to take your life?"

Arturo stood with slumped shoulders and downcast eyes. His face reflected his desperation. "There is absolutely nothing worth living for."

Without reproach but with a prayer to God for this frightened individual, Paul questioned him further. "Tell me your problem, Arturo; everybody wants to live. What happened?"

"Hermano Pablo, there is not one reason why I should live."

"That is not possible. No one wants to die. People spend their very last peso to stay alive when they are ill."

Arturo hemmed and hawed before his dilemma slowly surfaced. He admitted to fraudulent business dealings, facing a jail sentence, embittered enemies, lawsuits, almost losing his wife, his home, and everything he owned.

"I can't envision another solution other than ending my miserable life. I can't go on existing like this." Arturo grew more sullen.

Paul sought words of comfort to discourage Arturo from his determination to end it all, while Arthur strode around the room, nervously waving his revolver around.

Finally, Paul did something he had never done before (and doesn't recommend anyone doing, especially with a person contemplating suicide).

Impetuously, Paul obeyed a rash inspiration. "Arturo, I have the solution. Kill yourself!"

The man stopped his pacing and stared at Paul, incredulous. "Is that why you have come, Hermano Pablo?"

"No, Arturo, suicide is not a solution. On the contrary, suicide would be total destruction. Nevertheless, I want you to realize that there are two ways of committing suicide. The spineless way of ending your existence is putting the gun to your head and pulling the trigger. However, there is a dignified way that does not end in death. It is the assassination of your pride. Your problem, Arturo, is egotism, which keeps you from admitting your predicament, accepting responsibility of your guilt, paying your creditors, and even going to jail."

Arturo was obviously bewildered by Paul's clarification. "How does one commit suicide of one's pride?"

"It's impossible for you to commit suicide of your arrogance, Arturo. Only Jesus Christ living in your heart can give you the ability to do that."

"Explain how it is possible to invite Jesus into my heart." For the first time since Paul had entered the house, Arturo stopped pacing and no longer brandished his gun. The slightest spark of optimism seemed to grab hold of him.

"Arturo, would you be interested in inviting Jesus into your heart and permitting Him to eradicate your arrogance?"

"Yes. Yes!" Arturo placed his loaded handgun on a chair between them.

Paul explained the plan of salvation before asking this remorseful man to repeat a prayer inviting Jesus to be the Lord and guide of his life.

After solemnly repeating the prayer of invitation for Jesus to inhabit his heart, Arturo leaped to his feet and hurried to give Paul a bear hug that almost broke his ribs.

Jubilant, Arturo hurried from the room to inform his wife, who had just invited Jesus into her heart through the personal witnessing of Carlos Valiente's wife. The two new believers in Jesus Christ hugged each other happily. God's grace provided a joyful ending to a terrifying evening.

Paul returned to the Mancia home, ate a reheated dinner, and expressed gratitude that God had allowed him the privilege of leading Arturo to Christ.

Chapter 26
Rev. Norman Mydske Opens Doors of Ministry

The Rev. Norman Mydske, the representative of Billy Graham in Latin America, needed an orator for his crusades. Paul accepted the invitation as an open door for ministry that lasted for 40 years.

Norman Mydske, missionary to Peru, was the founder and director of Radio del Pacífico, with many repeater stations in that country.

He knew of Paul through La Iglesia del Aire ("The Church of the Air") program and in 1964 through Un Mensaje a la Conciencia ("A Message to the Conscience") radio programs.

In 1970 Rev. Mydske organized an evangelistic crusade in conjunction with the Alliance churches and invited Paul to be the speaker for the crusade held in the Plaza de Acho, the famous bull-fighting ring in the capital of Peru.

Attendance at the well-publicized Bull Ring crusade was surprisingly large. With 4,000 people registering a decision to make Jesus Christ the Lord of their lives, the acceptance of the gospel message made headline news.

Live phone-in television conversations brought Christ's message to the 4 million inhabitants of Lima each night after the crusade service. Most of the questions were relative to our relationship to Jesus Christ. Many thousands of lives were impacted with the story of salvation. Some callers expressed an adverse opinion of the evangelical message. Then immediately other callers begged forgiveness for the one who had said such a thing and asked Hermano Pablo to continue.

One afternoon Mydske arranged an interview for Paul in a hotel lobby with a reporter of a dubious local newspaper. The reporter began with the usual preliminary questions, and Paul waited patiently for the predictable trick question.

"Hermano Pablo, I've been to the Bull Ring and you speak very convincingly, but tell me, how does your message put food in the stomachs of the poor?"

Without hesitation, Paul began with a symbolic illustration that is the testimony of many people. "His name is Juan. He is an alcoholic incapable of holding down a job, consuming everything he earns. His companion with whom he has several children sells merchandise in the marketplace to put food on the table. His living quarters have no furniture and the children are without shoes. Often these young defenseless ones find their father in the gutter and help him stumble home.

"One day, as Juan staggered toward home in a drunken stupor, he came upon a group of people singing jubilantly, which enticed Juan, so he entered the building and sat in a backseat, absorbing the peaceful atmosphere. The pastor, who had formerly been a Juan, explained how God changed his way of life from one of slavery to alcohol to one of freedom and happiness. The pastor ended his persuasive message by inviting anyone who wanted deliverance of addictions to come to the altar."

The previously arrogant newspaper reporter by now had laid down his pad and pencil and was listening intently as Paul continued his narrative.

"Juan, the drunkard, stumbled forward, falling to his knees at the altar, humbly and earnestly agreeing with the pastor's entreaty that God would change Juan's life just as God had changed the pastor's life.

"Juan left the place of worship with alcohol on his breath but with an extraordinary feeling of hope inside him as he retraced his steps to his home. Entering meekly, not angrily and throwing his weight around as he usually did, his companion and children eyed him suspiciously. Because of Juan's strangely altered conduct, his partner became suspicious and insisted on knowing what had happened to him.

"'Are you sick?' she asked.

"Juan shook his head. 'I don't understand what has happened, but the pastor says I invited Jesus into my heart, and I don't think I'm ever going to drink again.'

"His long-suffering companion smirked. 'Ah, I've heard that story before.'

"Juan, true to his word, found employment, and on payday he brought the entire paycheck home to his companion, apologizing for not having done so before.

"Juan didn't drink again, his companion and children attended church, and they also accepted Christ as their Savior. Together they learned to read the Bible. The family now eats properly every day, they have furniture and the roof no longer leaks.

"One day Juan came home with a pail of paint to brighten their dwelling, something that had never entered his mind before. Juan began a very different lifestyle as a leader in the community. His children were healthy and educated. He enjoyed the hope of eternal life with God."

Now Paul asked the reporter. "You tell me if what I preach does or does not put food in the stomachs of the poor."

The newspaper reporter studied Paul for a moment. He crossed him arms on his chest and heaved a sigh. "Hermano Pablo, I am that Juan."

Genuinely sympathetic by the confession of the obviously miserable reporter, Paul urged him to accept Christ and allow Him to solve his problems.

With slumped shoulders and lowered eyes, the reporter shook his head. "No, I can't now. I have too many details to solve first."

Paul encouraged the man not to hesitate. "Give your problems to Christ; He wants to help you."

But the man left the hotel as he came, with the emptiness of heart only God can fill.

Rev. Mydske united pastors in working together a year in advance to prepare for crusade locations, choir, counselors, and local advertising. Dozens of the Mydske-organized crusades were in out-of-the-way places where most evangelists don't go. For Paul, all were "open doors" to share the story of Christ.

The 1987 Punta de Tralca, Chile, crusade was an interesting one. This was the very first time these churches had united for this type of event. One woman said it was the first time she had attended an evangelical gathering. The services were held in a park building. The accommodations for us and our singer, Fred Cancio, and his wife were in a Catholic monastery. They were the worst we've experienced in all our travels.

This first teaching congress for these leaders in Punta de Tralca was well received and the applauses and expressions of appreciation more than compensated for our physical sacrifices.

Paul became ill the last day, so Mydske hired a taxi to transport us to Santiago, the capital of Chile, for our plane trip home to California.

The following crusades in 1998 are samples of the many where Paul and Mydske ministered together. These four cities in Peru that we visited in one trip were difficult, especially because of the heat, but we were extremely blessed.

Piura, the third largest city in Peru, boasted a population of 1 million citizens. El Niño greeted us—the streets and even the coliseum were flooded, with watermarks 40-inches high. Men spent the entire day sweeping out water. We really didn't expect to have a service that night, but 2,000 people attended. The number doubled the next two nights, and 800 people made decisions to serve Christ.

The first floor of our hotel was also flooded, so we had to remove our shoes to walk in stocking feet through water from our room to the dining room.

The heat was overbearing. When Paul spoke to the pastors in the morning, the temperature and humidity was suffocating, but God's Holy Spirit was equally present.

Arequipa, at an altitude of 5,000 feet, is identified as the white city, because most of the buildings are made of white sandstone. We enjoyed a police escort everywhere we went, a blessing during heavy city traffic.

The coliseum held 10,000 people and was almost filled the first night. The 400 counselors were not prepared for the great spiritual harvest. The second night the coliseum was completely filled, something that no other Christian event had ever done. A total of 1,525 people accepted Christ as their Savior.

In the airport as we were leaving Arequipa, an airport guard brought a young atheist girl to Paul because she claimed she wanted to believe in God. Paul told her, "Read the Bible."

"But I don't believe the Bible," she responded.

"Read the Bible, anyway, even if you don't believe it," Paul insisted. "If you are sincere, God will reveal Himself to you."

Then before leaving the doubting girl, he took her hand and prayed that God would reveal Himself to her and that she would be obedient to His revelation.

Later the guard returned to report to Paul that the girl had told him, "That man left me feeling weak and thoughtful."

Pucalpa is a city on the Amazon River. Only aircraft or boat can reach it. Our so-called hotel suite, the best room of the hotel, was located directly above the kitchen fumes. It had two single-size beds, a tiny table, one chair, and a miniature refrigerator. The air conditioner didn't cool the room until the next morning.

The mayor wanted to introduce Hermano Pablo personally to the press, who were waiting in a conference room. The mayor opened a door to a large room full of people. The mayor presented Paul a document declaring him an illustrious and distinguished guest of Pucalpa.

One afternoon we were hit with a torrential downpour. It turned the reddish dirt into sticky mud, making it difficult to walk in. We weren't sure people could even get to the evening service, which was being held outside. In spite of this, some 4,000 attended the first service and 500 came forward for salvation. The head of Peru's Education Department also repeated the Sinner's Prayer. He was inspired to invite Paul to speak to 200 schoolteachers the next morning, resulting in half of them raising their hands for salvation.

We had police escorts everywhere we went, and two men sat outside our door all night to protect us from possible terrorists. They even roped off the platform for our protection and provided a police escort to keep us from being mobbed. The people wanted to touch, greet, pray with, or take a picture of their beloved "Message to the Conscience" radio communicator. The total harvest in Pucalpa was 1,704 people.

In Iquitos, the sweltering heat was an overbearing 100 degrees. This principal metropolis of Peru is situated on the Amazon River, an hour's flight from Pucalpa. City travel is almost entirely by two-seat (tricycle type) motorcycle carts that have an overhead awning and clear plastic coverings that can be lowered for protection from the rain.

The people took advantage of any opportunity to talk with Paul, even while we were eating. One after another came, shook hands and expressed their love and appreciation. Many people referred to him as the Evangelical Pope. Paul didn't let these manifestations of endearment go to his head.

Some 10,000 people filled the stadium in Iquitos, and another 10,000 stood outside. At the last minute, the brethren embarrassedly informed Paul that they didn't have lights in the stadium. Paul preached the first night with a pastor standing next to him shining a flashlight onto his Bible.

The next day the mayor was persuaded to send six lights to the stadium, sufficient to light the platform and steps. The Friday night service is difficult to describe. The semi-lit stadium was filled to capacity and some 500 crippled and ill people sat in wheelchairs or on the ground near the crusade platform.

The Lord manifested His presence in a powerful way. I was with Paul on the platform. At one point I got up in the semi-darkness to move from my place. I accidentally bumped Paul's arm as he prayed silently while Fred Cancio sang. It was like touching a live electric wire. I have never felt the presence of the Lord in such a powerful way.

When Paul finished his message, he paused a few seconds with his eyes closed before inviting the people to accept Christ. When he opened his eyes, the people were streaming down the aisles, almost running in the semi-darkness toward the platform to pray the Sinner's Prayer.

In spite of the anti-evangelical spirit in this region, or perhaps because of the numerous persecutions, 4,000 people in Iquitos found peace with God in the three days of the crusade.

Altogether, in the four crusades in out-of-the-way places that few evangelists visit, the harvest rendered 8,325 decisions for Christ.

Though this extended trip was physically exhausting, Paul's heart rejoiced because he was able to bring peace to many lost "Juans".

Chapter 27
Addicted to Prescription Drugs

Dear friends in Mexico City liberated me from sure destruction, when I suffered with constant headaches while taking prescription drugs prescribed by my medical doctor.

"Hermano Pablo, we would like to take you to our doctor." Idilio and Rosa Maria de Pardillo, my dental friends of Mexico City, offered.

That afternoon in 1976, Paul met a serious-faced homeopath doctor who queried him about everything he did, medications he took, and when he rested. Paul responded to each question frankly, while the doctor checked frequently in his guidebook and made notations on a writing pad.

After more than an hour of inquiries, he said, "Mr. Finkenbinder, I can help you, but my medication will have absolutely no effect unless you discontinue taking the medications you are now using." He handed Paul a vial of sugar granules impregnated with herbs. "Take ten granules daily."

Paul took the tiny container and left the office, praying the doctor's expertise in medicine was accurate.

Because our dear friends were paying the doctor for Paul's benefit, he promised to follow the doctor's instructions.

For years, Paul had been working frenetically, making two radio programs daily—one in Spanish and another in English—besides spending at least 100 days a year ministering in foreign countries. Life was one constant rushed activity. His ambitions drove him faster than he was physically capable, and he was always suffering with a splitting headache.

Years earlier Paul's medical doctor had sent him to Doctors Hospital in Beverly Hills, California, where for three days he was subjected to tests to try to find a tumor or cause of the constant pain. The resulting evaluation was that he had nothing abnormal. He was suffering from stress. He was given prescriptions for Equagesic and Valium. These pills brought blessed relief, however both drugs were addictive. Paul's activities were ever demanding. He had to increase the dosage to counteract the pain, and soon he became a drug addict, albeit with prescription drugs.

It was only by the grace of God that Paul was able to continue making radio programs. He saw the desire of Paul's heart and heard his cry for help, because it was on a trip to Puebla that God put it on the hearts of our friends Idilio and Rosa Maria to come to Paul's rescue. We never did learn how they discovered his addiction problem. Perhaps they saw it in his face and actions.

The night after preaching the evening message was the worst night of Paul's entire life. He had discontinued all the addictive medications. He obeyed the homeopathic doctor's mandate and took nothing for the pain, even though his head felt like it would burst. The wall of the hotel where he was staying was cement. In the night, he banged his head hard against the wall because that pain was less excruciating than the pain in his head. The next day the hurting had diminished somewhat, and each day after that the heretofore-unrelenting pain continued to subside.

When he arrived home a week later, I was amazed at Paul's youthful, revitalized appearance. No stress or anxiety lined his face. And he had no headache.

We don't know if the herb-impregnated sugar pills brought relief, or if it was getting off the addicting drugs that healed his body. In any case, without God's intervention he would have continued being a drug addict, probably getting worse every day.

Only God could have delivered him from that drug addiction and healed him of those horrible headaches that have never returned.

Chapter 28
Evangelism in Costa Rica & Honduras

*Paul, live on television, responded to the public every night
after the services in the stadium.*

Every night after the 1967 crusade service, Paul appeared
live on television for an hour in San Jose, Costa Rica.
This new facet of communication was of interest because a
Protestant was answering calls from Catholics.

Using Paul on television after the services was new. Even
though Costa Ricans were skeptical of the Protestant religion,
they were curious about it and asked questions every night.
Whenever a call criticized the Protestants, another caller would
defend them.

One woman left everyone in the television studio stunned
when she asked a question regarding the distinction between
evangelicals and the religion of the country.

"Hermano Pablo, I am Catholic, I attend Mass every day, and
I'm faithful to all the policies of the church, so why don't I have
peace in my heart?"

With a close up view of Paul live on television, and all Costa
Rica waiting for his response, you could have heard a pin drop
in the television studio. Paul remained serene, relying completely
on God's promise to give him answers when he needed them.

He congratulated the woman on her faithfulness to her church and then posed a question. "Is it possible you've made the customs of your church your god, instead of giving devotion to God Himself, who wants to be the object of your faith and dedication?"

The woman hesitated. "I never reflected on my daily devotion that way."

"Might you be interested in inviting Christ into your heart and giving Him the admiration and devotion you now give your liturgy?"

"Yes, I would."

Paul's heart rejoiced as he led and she repeated a prayer inviting Jesus to be the Lord of her life and the inspiration for her adoration.

The spiritual harvest in San Jose in 1967 was great, even though the sound in the stadium was far from good.

Later that week Paul accepted an invitation to the annual San Jose, Costa Rica, Presidential Prayer Breakfast. He entered the room and looked around for a place to sit. As he approached a table, Colonel José Maria Lemus, a past president of El Salvador, invited him to sit with him. They began chatting like old cronies.

Sitting at the same table with Colonel Lemus was a North American man by the name of William Bullard. Listening to Paul's conversation with the colonel, their mutual acquaintance, Bullard switched chairs and sat beside Paul, expressing surprise that he knew Colonel Lemus.

"Yes, I'm Paul Finkenbinder, also known as Hermano Pablo. I was a missionary in El Salvador where President Colonel Lemus entertained me a few times in his office.

Mr. Bullard didn't speak Spanish so Paul interpreted the activities of the prayer breakfast for him. Afterward they exchanged calling cards and said their good-byes.

The next January Paul received a letter from Mr. Bullard inviting him to the Presidential Prayer Breakfast in Washington, DC. Paul had already planned a crusade in Honduras in February and realized he could arrange the Presidential Prayer Breakfast in Washington, DC, as a plane stopover on the same trip. After acknowledging the invitation, Paul received a personal, printed invitation from President Johnson.

The breakfast in Washington, DC, was a huge event, and Paul's assigned table was far away from the podium. He took note of the 20 vice presidential guests at the President's table on the platform. Paul became excited, believing it God ordained, when he heard the name of Dr. Napoleon Alcerro, vice president of Honduras, the country where Paul was going.

The vice-presidential luncheon was at another hotel where vice president Hubert Humphrey was speaking. Paul was determined to meet Dr. Alcerro. He went to the hotel and when the luncheon had ended, Paul rushed to the doorway through which everyone had to file and startled the vice president with a Spanish salutation. He extended his hand in a warm handshake and asked, "Have you heard of the radio program *Un Mensaje a la Conciencia* (A Message to the Conscience)?

Dr. Alcerro's eyes grew wide. "Are you Hermano Pablo? Imagine meeting Hermano Pablo here. This is incredible."

Paul explained he was on his way to Honduras for crusades. Dr. Alcerro expressed sincere delight that Hermano Pablo was going to his country, and right then he gave Paul his vice-presidential office phone number as well as his home phone number.

Paul's plans took him first to Santa Rosa de Copan and then San Pedro Sula before going to Tegucigalpa, the capital of Honduras. When Paul visited Dr. Alcerro, the vice president questioned him. "Hermano Pablo, how come you have been in Honduras three weeks and just now are coming to see me?"

Surprised that Dr. Alcerro knew his itinerary, Paul asked, "How do you know how long I've been in your country and where I've been?"

The vice president smiled. "It's my business to know where you've been, what you've been doing, and how you've been behaving yourself." He went on to say that his wife, family, and many others of his Cabinet officials started each day with Hermano Pablo's four-minute radio "Message to the Conscience" broadcasts.

This was Monday morning. Paul invited Dr. Alcerro to a special Hotel Tea for Professionals that had been arranged for that afternoon.

"Excellent, Hermano Pablo, I'd love to attend. Is it all right if a few of my associates accompany me to your reception?"

"Of course, Dr. Alcerro."

Immediately the vice president began phoning friends, inviting them to the event. By his tone, he demanded their attendance.

Many of his friends attended. Near the end of the reception, Paul approached Dr. Alcerro and his colleagues, who were engaged in a serious discussion. "Gentlemen, are you deliberating the solution of the world's problems?"

"No, we're endeavoring to solve the problem of getting you to attend a gathering of Catholic Youth Leaders who are meeting tonight in a church."

"Dr. Alcerro, I'd really enjoy being there, but my own stadium conference is from 7:30 to 9 tonight."

"You must address our youth leaders tonight, Hermano Pablo." The entire group of men insisted imploringly.

"Tell me how I can possibly be present at your meeting from 7 to 8."

Dr. Alcerro spoke for the group. "When you die and God asks you about this speaking opportunity to 400 Catholic teachers of our young people, what will your answer be?"

Paul chuckled. "Very well, I'll shorten my message, and you can extend your meeting. Please have a car ready to pick me up at 8:30."

Another minister concluded the evangelistic service in the stadium for Paul as he rushed to the Catholic gathering; there he entered a cigarette smoke-filled room. A few nuns were present, but the audience was mostly made up of 400 men.

A lanky priest directed Paul to the center podium, announcing, "Hermano Pablo, we're delighted you are here to speak to us."

Rejoicing in his heart for the opportunity to witness for his Lord to these Catholic leaders, Paul began by telling them about a recent dream. In Paul's dream Jesus had returned to the earth, taken his parents and siblings, and left him because he had been disobedient to home responsibilities.

He continued speaking and made the application regarding the need of Jesus being the Lord of our lives, with the necessity of living righteous, exemplary lives before our young people, and being ready when Christ returns. When he ended speaking, he realized 20 minutes had passed.

The group applauded jubilantly as he left the podium. Even after he sat down, they stood and continued applauding at least five more minutes.

Several men congratulated Paul. A medical doctor gave him his calling card with this handwritten message: "Thank you, Hermano Pablo, for helping us see ourselves as we are." He signed his name.

Paul, extremely tired after the long day of activities, left the meeting, giving thanks to God for the opportunity of proclaiming the good news of salvation to a new group of people.

Never, in all his years of ministry in the Spanish world, did Paul keep a diary of conversions, breakfasts, television interviews or conversations with individuals—all occasions to share the message of Christ.

In a stadium, a convent, or a Catholic church, Paul is always ready to speak about Jesus Christ.

Chapter 29
A Suggestion that Blessed Peru

God responded to the prayers of the Peruvians
when they united in prayer.

"Hermano Pablo, what can we do?" lamented Rev. Pedro Ferreira, General Director of the Christian station Radio del Pacífico in Lima, Peru. "Our people are panicky and terrified by the terrorists. Today they bombed the hotel where you are registered to stay tonight, and they have threatened to poison the city's water supply. We don't know where to turn, or what to do."

It was midnight in Lima, Peru, when we arrived from Los Angeles on American Airlines. We were weary in body and hardly expected this sort of greeting. In anguish, even before starting the car that would take us to our hotel, Pedro expressed his terrifying fears for his country.

Paul turned his distraught face upward in prayer, seeking reassuring words for Pedro. Then gazing into Pedro's strained countenance, he asked, "Brother, you manage a radio station with satellite stations covering all of Peru, don't you? What would you think of beginning each day with a prayer service on your network of radio stations, asking God for His divine deliverance?"

"That sounds like a brilliant suggestion I had not considered." Pedro readily accepted the counsel.

163

More than a year passed before the "Morning Prayer" program began on May 7, 1989. The daily 30-minute 6 a.m. radio program blanketed the whole country of Peru. Ministers of different Christian denominations came to the station on selected days and led in prayers, asking God to answer on behalf of Peru. Miraculously, the frightening conditions in Peru—the fears, the economic crisis, and terrorism—began to change.

Many churches began holding weekly prayer meetings where several hundred Peruvians gathered to invoke God's deliverance. Paul and I attended the Lima church, where Pedro and his family attended Thursday all-night prayer services. Some 400 people stayed on their knees until 4 a.m., seeking the face of God. We were moved by the genuine godly devotion and dedication of those Peruvian people; we have never heard more beautiful prayers than these brethren elevated to the throne of God.

In 1993 Pedro invited Paul to speak at the third anniversary celebration of the National Movement of Prayer, which resulted from the early "Morning Prayer" programs. The stadium held 45,000 people and was filled to capacity. The overflow crowd of thousands more stood outside.

Dr. Ferreira expressed his sentiments. "God is good, because His mercy is forever. Peru has seen and continues to see great changes by the power of prayer. The evangelical believers in the decade of the 1990s have grown from two percent to 12 percent, and there are conversions in every service. Peru now has a stable economy with an abundance of earth-produced foods. It is possible to buy 35 small breads for a dollar because God responds to the prayers of His people."

Without doubt, it was the Holy Spirit of God who inspired Paul to suggest a "Morning Prayer" program. Dr. Ferreira united the Peruvian people to pray together as one body for God to bless their country.

Chapter 30
A Renewed Vision in El Chaco, Paraguay

*Paul stood in the sun before a vast group of Indians. He saw
the same brown-colored faces he had seen in a vision at Zion
Bible School when he was only 17 years of age.*

Descendents of Mennonites who migrated from Germany
to South America at the beginning of the 20th century
invited us to Asuncion, Paraguay, in 1999. They had built a dozen
Christian schools and a 5,000-seat stadium called the Guttenberg,
where special events, such as ours, brought rejoicing for three
days, with pastors who came for a time of spiritual refreshing.

The evening services were the best organized we have ever
attended in any country, with a beautiful spirit of unity among
all the pastors. Paul ministered daily to the pastors who had traveled from their homes from every area of Paraguay. In the three-
night evangelistic services with pastors, we witnessed over 300
first-time decisions for Christ.

One message titled "Renew in Me" ended with three hours
of prayer, repentance, and dedication to God for renewed fervor
to serve the Master.

Early Sunday morning, we were taken on a 90-minute flight
in a single engine plane, to Filadelfia in the Chaco area near the
Bolivian border. Several carloads of people left Asuncion at 3

a.m. to make the six-hour trip in time for the 10 a.m. morning service in Filadelfia.

Some 600 serious-faced pastors filled the church. These men sat quietly, seemingly unresponsive to the message Paul gave on God's Mosaic in which he emphasized the value of each person and how God wants and needs every person just as they are. When Paul finished his message, Rev. Arnold Weins, our host, gave Paul's hand a quick squeeze, indicating that his words were what these calloused, sun-bathed Indian men needed to hear.

After the message that assured them that God loved them as they are, the pastors stood patiently in line to shake our hands. It was a moving experience to look into the eyes of these bronze-skinned, wrinkle-faced men of faith with broken teeth and calloused hands, whose ancestors had been savages, but now our brothers in Christ.

The afternoon service held in the open air under the hot tropical sun had a minimum of 6,000 people representing six or seven different dialect tribes of Indians. Many of them had traveled from distant villages, walking for two days to meet Hermano Pablo, who had blessed them with "A Message to the Conscience" program for 24 years.

The Mennonite radio station, the Lighthouse, that everyone listened to, was the first in that area to broadcast the four-minute spiritual program.

Paul's message that afternoon was about the Samaritan woman whom Jesus told about the living water. When Paul invited those who wanted to drink of that same living water to come forward, hundreds flocked to the area in front of the platform to partake of Jesus' living water.

After the service, as we rested in a motel room, Paul held back tears as he told me of the panorama he saw before him. "This afternoon tears stung my eyes and my throat constricted when I saw with my eyes the same bronze faces I saw in my vision at Zion. Before me today, I relived the vision I saw of the forlorn, brown-skinned people who called out to me in desperation, 'You have something to give us; please don't deny us.'"

Interestingly, the countries of Bolivia and Peru, which border Paraguay, are the countries where Hermano Pablo's program is perhaps appreciated the most. In addition, it is the precise region where Paul had his friend put his picture on a map of South America when God gave him the vision of faces at Zion when he was only 17. In Bolivia and in Peru, on radio, television, and in print, "A Message to the Conscience" program is transmitted almost 5,000 times daily, doubling that of any other countries.

A myriad of heartrending brown-skinned faces renewed the vision God gave Paul when he was a young student in Zion Bible Institute many years ago.

Chapter 31
Paul's Life is Threatened

Paul doesn't run away frightened by dreaded situations.
His only fear is not fulfilling God's divine purpose for his life.

NEWS ALERT!
A LATE NEWS BULLETIN FROM EL SALVADOR, CEN-
TRAL AMERICA, REPORTS THAT MISSIONARY REV.
PAUL FINKENBINDER, KNOWN AS **HERMANO PABLO**
IN HIS INTERNATIONAL RADIO BROADCASTS IS
MISSING. LINDA, HIS WIFE, HAS RETURNED TO THE
UNITED STATES WITHOUT HIM.

Jumping from bed, frightened and trembling from a vivid
nightmarish dream that held this news report, Ethel, our
blind sister-in-law in Denver, Colorado, insisted that her blind
husband, George, call his brother Paul. Ethel became extremely
distraught when we acknowledged that we had accepted an invitation to be in El Salvador for the Easter sunrise services. She
was persuaded that her vivid dream was a God-given forewarning
for us not to make the trip to El Salvador.

Paul assured Ethel and his brother, George, that he would take
every security precaution possible and never allow himself to be
alone. This in no way negated my petrifying fears of kidnappers

or an enemy bullet finding its target; nevertheless, my supplications to abandon the trip plans fell on deaf ears.

Recent newspaper headlines screamed the tragic death of Archbishop Romero. Since Hermano Pablo was the most prominent Protestant evangelical, he became their next target. The conditions in El Salvador, where our family had lived peacefully for 21 years, had changed to one of hostility and violence. Terrorists stole cars daily and used them to commit all manner of crimes—merciless murders, plundering, and kidnappings—and then deserted the crime vehicles on any street for the owners to find.

Regardless of these frightening conditions, Paul had accepted the year before an invitation to speak at the Easter sunrise service on April 6, 1980.

John Bueno, our missionary colleague residing in San Salvador, recommended that we not make the trip because of the violence in the country. At the same time, the Christian radio station committee begged us not to cancel our travels, because there was great anticipation for Hermano Pablo's arrival.

We didn't alarm our children by telling them of their Aunt Ethel's dream. We did feel uneasy just before leaving for the airport, so Paul called our friend, the Rev. Ralph Wilkerson, and asked for prayer.

That night at 8 p.m., while we were in flight to Central America, the Wilkerson's were traveling on the freeway. Ralph's wife, Allene, suddenly felt a disturbing fear for our lives. They stopped the car to pray for our protection.

At the same time, during the regular plane stop in Guatemala, John Bueno tried unsuccessfully to reach us by phone at the Guatemalan airport to tell us to discontinue our travel to El Salvador.

When the plane landed in San Salvador at 10:30 p.m., our hosts were at the ramp of the plane to meet us. Because Paul was celebrated and appreciated in that country and had received the key to the city by the mayor on a previous visit, we didn't find it odd to see them there; however, what did startle us was that a military guard carrying a submachine gun should accompany them.

This special concession at the foot of the plane was to warn us that the radio station had received several calls threatening that Paul's life would end that night if he attempted to enter San Salvador.

We remembered our sister-in-law's dream of my returning to the United States without Paul. My heart pounded in fear as I imagined a jillion uncertainties. How could we possibly be safe in a land of evil terrorists?

As we entered the airport seven guards, all with submachine guns, dispatched by the military, surrounded Paul. I walked outside the circle. This unusual commission of guards was to protect the well-known Hermano Pablo around the clock; however long he stayed in the country and wherever he went, they were always to surround him.

Authorities directed us to a tiny room. The seven guards remained outside the door while Paul, the welcoming committee, and I held hands and prayed for God's direction. As we prayed, someone came with a message that Paul should call John Bueno. This was a special concession granted only for VIPs, because travelers cannot make or receive phone calls before going through immigration.

Paul called John Bueno, who said the situation was extremely serious. "Paul, I can't divulge over the phone how I'm familiar with the terrorist's plans to kill you tonight, but I strongly urge you to return to the plane and fly anywhere it goes."

My heart almost stopped beating, and nausea churned in my stomach as I stood silently in a corner of the tiny room, anxiously praying that Paul would agree to leave.

"God, direct me," I heard Paul praying audibly. "I can't run away from this responsibility because I'm terrified. Several members of this welcoming committee do not believe the terrorists' threats."

Uncertain of what to do and desiring the conformity of the entire group, Paul impulsively tore six sheets off a small pad of paper he found on the desk. He handed a paper to each of our five friends and one to me. "Write down yes if we are to stay, or no if we are to leave." He sat silently waiting for our votes.

Paul told me later, "My heart pounded madly as I counted three yes votes to remain and three no votes to leave, but adding John Buenos's dissenting vote, I knew I was supposed to leave."

An airline employee quickly advised the pilot of the waiting plane of our decision to depart; another agent sent for our luggage, while another quickly prepared visas for Panama City, the plane's next stop. These extraordinary concessions, including holding up a plane for Hermano Pablo, were highly unusual.

The seven guards with submachine guns encircled Hermano Pablo as we retraced our steps to the ramp of the plane. Before bidding farewell to our radio-station friends, Paul said a prayer for them and the guards. Two guards, machine guns poised, dutifully followed us up the ramp steps, providing protection until we entered the plane. They waited on the tarmac until the door closed.

The flight attendant wore a curious look as she took us to our previous seats. "Who are you, and what is all the commotion about?" she asked.

Our heart's raced as we explained the death threat against Hermano Pablo, the popular "A Message to the Conscience" radio broadcast host.

Two verses of our beloved Psalm 91 elevated our spirits, comforting and revitalizing our trembling bodies as the airplane took us away from the terrorists. "Because he loves me, the Lord says, I will rescue him; I will protect him, for he acknowledges my Name. He will call upon me, and I will answer him; I will be with him in trouble, I will deliver him and honor him" (Ps. 91:14-15).

While walking into the Panama airport, physically exhausted and thanking God for His protection of our lives, we were again terrified as airport speakers blasted an announcement requesting that Hermano Pablo pick up a page telephone. Had the terrorists accompanied us to Panama?

Paul wiped his moist hands on his pants then picked up a courtesy phone. Evidently, one of our Salvadoran airport friends had called evangelist Richard Jeffery, who was holding a crusade in Panama City. Jeffery and his wife, Elva, had been our house-guests during the three months of the San Salvador crusade in 1955. Now they were waiting for us at the airport to host us for the night.

The next morning, weary in body after a restless and sleepless night but grateful for God's divine protection, we flew to Miami and from there back to California. We were thankful to be home safely.

By the miraculous mercy of God, Paul's life was spared from certain death.

Chapter 32
A Macedonian Call

Hermano Pablo planted a spiritual seed
in the Dominican Republic, and after many days,
it returned with multiple blessings.

We returned from a crusade service in Monterrey, Mexico, in 1997 to discover a small business card on the floor inside our Holiday Inn motel door. Puzzled, Paul picked up the card, which bore the printed name of Dr. Gilberto Velez. As he pondered who this could be, he read the scribbled words, "Please call me; we met in the Dominican Republic."

Paul flipped the card over and was surprised to recognize his own scrawled handwriting: "One day I will lay down my tools; you take them and follow my example." It was obviously a memo from a former trip.

The next morning, Paul phoned Dr. Velez and made an appointment to have lunch with him. To our joy and surprise, Gilberto was one of the medical students we met 16 years earlier while ministering in the Dominican Republic in 1981. Upon seeing the announcement of Hermano Pablo's Monterrey meetings and learning that he came from Laredo, Texas, Gilberto paid a Holiday Inn employee $20 to put his calling card under our door.

Seeing Gilberto brought back memories of our association in San Pedro de Macoris, Dominican Republic. Gilberto and a half dozen Christian medical students, burdened for the spiritual welfare of fellow students, had the inspiration to invite Hermano Pablo for a crusade on their island. The students had admitted: "We are embarrassed to tell you that we have no funds, we cannot pay your airfare, nor the hotel or stadium, but the need is great. Would you come to the Dominican Republic and speak to us?

Paul remembered the invitation from this little group known as AMEC, who explained how they met together regularly for prayer out of concern for the spiritual welfare of the 16,000 university students. The students came from all over the world, including Cuba and Lebanon, and even a Hindu princess attended, who arrived for her classes in a chauffeured limousine. Some students were very poor, many living in cramped quarters but studying diligently in preparation for their desired vocations.

The letter from the AMEC group laid on Paul's desk many days as together the staff and we prayed and deliberated how to respond, because Hermano Pablo Ministries had no funds either. Nevertheless, Hermano Pablo's heart wouldn't allow him to deny these young people burdened for the salvation of other medical students, who would be doctors in all parts of the world.

Paul accepted the challenging invitation of these courageous young people, set a date, and requested that they make a reservation for the two of us in a nearby hotel.

Some of the local pastors of the Dominican Republic were appalled by the audacity of the young students for daring to invite Hermano Pablo for a crusade, with no promise of any funds. The same pastors went so far as to ridicule these students.

Undaunted, the ambitious Christian medical students promoted the evangelistic crusade every way they could. One sympathetic friend took a week off work, donating his time to hand out invitations from house to house and posting flyers on street corners. Gilberto reminded us that this young person had been our driver, making several trips to the airport from the town of Macoris for our luggage that American Airlines had lost for three days.

The founding president of the Universidad Central del Este (Central University of the East), Dr. Josue Hazin Azar, was not interested in evangelicals and didn't pay attention to the AMEC group. However, when Dr. Azar learned that Hermano Pablo was a Rotarian, he invited Paul to his office and received him with kindness. Not only did he open the University for an Evening Service, he even paid for the crusade stadium, our hotel, and the car rental—with only one requirement: that Hermano Pablo attend a Rotary meeting as his guest.

Several hundred people accepted Christ in the Dominican Republic. Equally important to Paul were the personal contacts, television interviews, radio talk shows, and newspaper coverage. One evening Paul conversed two hours with a young student who couldn't comprehend God's never-ending love.

Today many of these medical students—friends of Gilberto—are renowned surgeons and specialists in diverse fields of medicine in different parts of the world.

After the joyful recounting of the past, we learned that Gilberto and his wife, Zulma, who also had been one of the AMEC prayer group, were now both medical doctors in San Antonio, Texas.

Although a practicing medical doctor, Gilberto also served as an assistant pastor of two Hispanic churches in San Antonio. He still carried in his billfold the note Hermano Pablo had given him in the Dominican Republic—the one he'd placed under our door: "One day I will lay down my tools; you take them and follow my example"—and said he felt God's call on his life.

After seven years in San Antonio, Gilberto and Zulma accepted the pastorate of a tiny nucleus of believers in Laredo,

Texas. The group soon outgrew their church facilities. When Paul and I visited that expanding group of believers in 2003, they were constructing a sanctuary for 3,300 people. Gilberto says he replicated Paul's example of making a first-class edifice when he constructed his $6 million lighthouse as a soul-winning tool for God. In June 2005 we attended the inauguration of the beautiful imposing structure Iglesia Misericordia, "Mercy Church" in northern Laredo, a relatively small city on the U.S.-Mexican border.

Paul wonders if he had disregarded the invitation of those moneyless medical students, would the highly talented Gilberto be serving God today.

Chapter 33
Zacchaeus

Like Zacchaeus, the biblical personage, a sad dejected man wanted to know Jesus. He came to Paul, beseeching him that his family might know Him too.

Paul was standing near the exit of the Missionary Alliance church in Mexico City, greeting a seemingly endless line of people who had attended the service.

A fashionable, heavyset woman detained the extended procession of greeters to ask Paul if he would speak to her atheist son. Paul wasn't the least bit interested in speaking to an atheist; however, he graciously informed the mother that perhaps he'd have the opportunity at some future time.

"He's standing next to me." She reached her arm around her fine-looking, well-dressed lawyer son and presented him to Paul.

Paul had no way to evade him. He extended his hand in a warm handshake. "So, you are an atheist?"

The man proudly nodded his head.

Paul looked straight into the eyes of the admitted unbeliever. "There are two different categories of agnostics. One is the agnostic who truthfully would like to believe in God but doesn't have faith in Him because it contradicts his logical nature. The second maintains he is agnostic because it allows him to consider himself significantly important. I need to know before we continue our discussion, which of the two agnostics are you?"

Paul's straightforward approach obviously surprised the man. He cleared his throat and shrugged his shoulders. "I admit that I'm the second kind."

Appreciating his honesty, Paul responded kindly, "When you are interested in God, I'd be delighted to converse with you."

The egotistical attorney acknowledged Paul politely and shook his hand. Taking his mother's arm, he exited the church without additional comment. Paul continued to greet the remaining attendees.

Paul had used three illustrations for the evangelistic message that evening, "All that Christ wants from us is hunger." His three biblical examples were: 1) the adulterous woman, representing the base sector of life; 2) Nicodemus, the professional/theological sector; and 3) Zacchaeus, the executive.

When Zacchaeus climbed a tree, he demonstrated curiosity, hunger, and sincerity to see the Savior. The theme of the message was that Jesus always sees the genuine hunger in a man's life. He looks beyond outward labels of Catholicism or Protestantism and meets the heart's deepest need.

The last person waiting patiently in the long line of greeters was a man with penetratingly dark, sad eyes. With shoulders slumped, he said, "I'm Zacchaeus, and I'd like to invite you to my house."

"I'm uncertain if my agenda will allow me the time," Paul responded.

"But Jesus went to Zacchaeus' house."

There was no mistaking that this businessman was miserable. Still gripping Paul's extended hand, he pleaded, "My sister heard you speak in Los Mochis last year, and Father Lomoli told my daughter, Anita, that I'd find a solution to my troubles if I could find you, Hermano Pablo. I've attended all your services this weekend and they have helped me tremendously, because I am like the hungry and needy Zacchaeus you were talking about in your message." His eyes, dark pools of sadness, stared deeply into Paul's. "Please, Hermano Pablo, will you come to my home in Saltillo and share this message with my people?"

The passion of this man's pleading heart was so sincere and his request was so earnest that Paul took this Zacchaeus', whose real name was Santos Barrera, address and promised to visit him in far-away Saltillo.

A few weeks after returning to Costa Mesa, Hector Tamez, Paul's ministry companion, made a trip to Saltillo to arrange for Paul's visit. Much to the surprise of Hector, our Zacchaeus had brought together 16 Catholic priests to interview him. One of them candidly asked, "Who are you, and who is Hermano Pablo? Why does he want to come to Saltillo? Is he Catholic or Protestant?"

"Neither," Hector responded without hesitation. "Hermano Pablo is a Christian, and his only desire is to speak about Jesus."

Afterward, one of the priests told Hector that he'd been praying that some priest in Saltillo would have the desire to speak only about Jesus.

Santos Barrera obtained a large conference room for Hermano Pablo's visit to Saltillo. Another person brought folding chairs, and a neighborhood Catholic Church lent its public-address system for the occasion—all in a spirit of unity. A benevolent woman served soft drinks for refreshments every night.

Paul arrived on Tuesday and found 700 people crowded into the conference room built for 500. A Catholic bishop, six priests, and various Protestant ministers expectantly sat on the front row. Paul's first words were to reassure everyone that he had no plan or desire to change anyone's religion, yearning only that every person there would have peace with God.

Almost everyone—including the six priests and the bishop—stood at the conclusion of the message to repeat the Sinner's Prayer. It was so spontaneous that Paul believed they had misunderstood the commitment they were making. So he had them sit while he explained the plan of salvation again. When he repeated the invitation, the same people stood to receive Christ as their Savior.

The third night Paul recognized faces of those who had stood before and this gave him the opportunity to clarify that it wasn't necessary to accept Christ repeatedly. One time is sufficient because eternal salvation is by the divine grace of God.

By the time Hermano Pablo left Saltillo, the group planned Bible study groups, using the Bible as the textbook, and meetings for prayer in both the Catholic and Protestant churches.

A Dr. Roberto Huereca promised to put the "Message to the Conscience" radio program on two radio stations and in a column in their local newspaper.

Our Zacchaeus, Santos Barrera, personally sponsored our program on another radio station in Saltillo.

Santos's children asked Paul, "What did you do to our father? Since he returned from Mexico City, he is a different man. He is no longer depressed. Now he reflects peace and tranquility."

Santos, wanting his family to hear Hermano Pablo's message, insisted Paul sleep in his bed in Saltillo. He didn't want the sheets changed afterward; hoping some of Pablo's qualities would rub off on him.

Paul has known a number of Catholic priests who were desirous of knowing more about God. One youth studying for the priesthood in Santa Ana, El Salvador, had established a friendship with missionaries Melvin and Lois Hodges. After many conversations and examining Scriptures, he wanted to escape the convent where he was living.

By previous arrangements, Paul parked our car around the corner near the convent. The student exited quickly and got into the backseat of our car. He lay on the floor while we drove him to the airport. He flew to Los Angeles to study in the Bible School in La Puente, California. Later he became pastor of an evangelical church in California.

Another priest hungry to know more about the Scriptures used to come to our house at night in San Salvador. We would turn off all lights in front of the house and the living room so he and Paul could discuss Scriptures for extended lengths of time.

Paul always opened his heart to speak with any person desirous to know the peace of God.

Chapter 34
A Nervous Collapse

God detained the energetic Paul in his mad aspiration
to evangelize all Latin America.

"Doctor, it is imperative that I make this trip to Ecuador. It has been planned for over a year."

"You have shingles, Paul. I'll give you a prescription for the pain." The doctor began writing on his pad. With only a glance at the rash forming a line from the center of Paul's chest to the center of his back, the doctor had immediately diagnosed his condition.

"Shingles is tantamount to a fuse blowing before a complete nervous collapse," the doctor continued. He could tell that Paul was not accepting his diagnosis, so he asked him to come see him before he left on his trip, knowing he would be bedridden instead.

Paul left the clinic preoccupied with the extreme pain but more especially that the doctor gave him no assurance regarding his trip to Ecuador.

That year of 1982 had been extremely busy for Paul. Besides the production of his radio and television programs, he had ministered 100 days in Honduras, Mexico, and Bolivia.

The Christmas holidays were nearing, and Paul—always the enthusiastic leader—lost all interest in festivities because the painful sores had increased around his chest to his back. It was unbearably agonizing for him even to lie in bed. It didn't take long for Paul to comprehend the horror of shingles and that it would be impossible for him to go to Ecuador. He cancelled all travels for 1983.

Fortunately, his friend Elmer Bueno, also an evangelist, had a cancellation and was available to take Paul's place in Cuenca. Later, Paul agreed that Elmer's acceptance and success in Cuenca was proof that no one is indispensible in God's work.

In constant pain, on January 6 in the middle of the night while Elmer was in Cuenca, Ecuador, Paul penned the revelation God showed him regarding the madness of his life and ministry.

"Lord, I have never cancelled an evangelistic campaign, and while I have been suffering in my bed, I've reflected on the activities of my life and my priorities. For more than 10 years, my constant frustration has been the many trips: making plans, packing suitcases, standing in long airplane lines, sitting in tight seats with people talking constantly. In addition, all this after being extremely tired from making radio and television programs in advance of the trip.

"Ministry is satisfying once I am at my destination and settled in a hotel, which I also detest, but at least I can shut the door and be alone. In Tegucigalpa and San Pedro Sula, Honduras, in April last year, I had three to five obligations each day, not counting the evening services. In Santa Cruz, Bolivia, I preached 20 times in seven days, not counting interviews and counseling. If only my singer, Fred Cancio, and I could be transported on a magic carpet to these crusade places, then I could continue.

"Please, God, forgive me for feeling upset at all this activity of trips after I had promised to give you my life. Help me to obediently travel wherever you want me to go.

I love radio and television, and since starting radio in 1955, I have never been bored preparing programs or felt distress because it was time to record another program. Television is a most dynamic way to minister and I always look forward to the pre-arranged days for recording the programs. Therefore, God, why can't I serve you by just producing radio and television programs? Why is it obligatory to travel so constantly?

"These frustrating questions have been going around in my tormented mind, revealing my wild life of activities, and for the first time I'm understanding the confusion I am in.

"God, do you mean to tell me that I have brought all this frustration upon myself? Are you saying I don't have to travel constantly? Is it possible that I can leave some of the travel, conferences, board memberships, and crusades to others?

"God revealed that it was the demands of men that are killing me. I thought I needed to make sacrifices to please God. Mistake! By the grace of God, he stopped me in my wild rush and I came down with shingles instead of suffering a complete nervous collapse. Nothing in my 61 years of life has had such positive liberation as this physical detention. I am free to relax, to enjoy a sabbatical, to say no, to get off many boards. I am very thankful that the Lord will allow me to make radio and television programs without constant travel.

"One night after God saw me through this entire maze I penned the following poem:

WHAT FOR THE RUSH

I'm rushing mad through life, with motives pure.
I'm doing things my peers call "right," "secure."
I've many friends that back me all the way,
And yet, with all the clap, I'm left affray.
But isn't rushing what it's all about?
Must we not from the housetops give our shout?
Then what's this sense of emptiness I feel?
Where is the joy that rushing should reveal?
I must not let these silly thoughts come in.
For after all, without the rush, I sin.
So on I run, making the "race" the "goal,"
Not seeing that the "rush" is "not the whole."
What's that I hear my whispering thoughts to say?
That rushing, running mad is not the way?
"Thoughts, to one side, I've much too much to do,
And time's against me, so away with you.
For isn't rushing what it's all about?"
Why does this question, then, so loudly shout?
Have I somehow, someway missed some fine truth?
If not the rush, then, what's the final proof?
I posed the quest as honestly as could.
I pondered all the sides I thought I should,
And then began to see I'd missed the mark.
That rushing is not the goal but just the start.
Somewhere along life's path, I got confused.
"The purpose is the rush," within I mused.
How wrong I was. The race is not the goal.
The goal is rest, and peace, and calm of soul."

God's ultimate intention for mankind in the words of His Son, Jesus, declares *"Peace I leave with you, my peace I give unto you: not as the world giveth, give I unto you. Let not your heart be troubled, neither let it be afraid"* (John 14:27 KJV).

REFLECTION

"When you, my colleague, are frustrated by one facet
> of your ministry, as successful as you may be,
> this will have a devastating effect on your
> whole life and the following will happen:

"The fulfilling side of your ministry will never reach
> its maximum potential.

"The frustration you feel will negatively affect your
> ministry accomplishments.

"You will be bored and tired all the time in that area
> of ministry that is frustrating you.

"It will be hard to have open, free, spontaneous
> fellowship with the Lord.

"Peer pressure will enslave you. What people think of
> you and your ministry will totally dominate
> your mind.

"Your whole life will be a confusing maze. You will
> not be able to arrange proper priorities for your
> life.

"You will be constantly dragging yourself through life
> instead of flowing freely.

"You will become critical and bitter at others who
> seem to have a lot of time on their hands—
> more than you feel you can afford.

"You will be continually worn out physically.

"Your rest and leisure times will be as filled with rush
and frustration as your work times.

"You will never relax completely.

"Your family will suffer the confusion that you have.

"Your most important relationship is with God, which
will affect your faith, confidence, and
dependence in Him."

Chapter 35
Cuenca, Ecuador

Several times Hermano Pablo has visited Cuenca,
a beautiful city high in the mountains of Ecuador.

In 1970 Paul first visited the beautiful city of Cuenca, Ecuador, situated 9,000 feet above sea level. At that time the population was a half a million people and the city had only 60 Christians.

On another visit to the city of universities, Paul had the honor of inaugurating the new House of Culture Theater in the center of the city. The theater was filled to capacity from the first night.

The two television stations fought over which station would air the live call-in night program after the service in the House of Culture. They finally settled on both of them airing the programs, which resulted in the spectacular 2,500 decisions for Christ in five days.

A group attempted to obstruct the increased impact the evangelicals made in Cuenca. They managed to rent the theater one evening prior to the crusade time and detained the closing of their service by prolonged singing of hymns. Finally, they vacated the building.

Six nuns had stayed behind when their group left. "Hermano Pablo, may we stay to hear your message?" they asked.

"By all means," he replied. He warmly shook hands with each one, reassuring them they were welcome to listen to his message while hidden behind the platform curtains.

In 2001 Paul was invited to be the speaker at the 11th anniversary celebration of the Assemblies of God Christian Center.

Missionaries Bill and Connie McDonald gave their perspective of the event:

"More than 9,000 people filled the coliseum for the celebration on Sunday morning. The service began with a parade of representatives from the 19 churches that the Christian Center church had founded. The children were dressed in typical Indian costumes; the boys were painted with mustaches to appear as adults.

"Paul's message using four biblical illustrations emphasized that Jesus still desires to help hurting people. The four points were the woman adulterer (Jesus doesn't condemn), Zacchaeus (Jesus changes lives), the woman with the blood hemorrhage (Jesus responds to a touch), and Lazarus who had been dead for four days (Christ can resurrect a dead situation).

"When Paul gave the invitation for those who wanted to invite that same Jesus into their hearts, the people came forward spontaneously, almost crowding to be first. The pastors cried while moving chairs back from the platform area to make room for the many aching Cuenca citizens longing to make contact with the Jesus of the Bible. There were 200 altar counselors, but they were inadequate to handle the crowd because more than 3,200 people repeated the Sinner's Prayer and received evangelistic literature as they exited the building. (Everyone had to exit through one door, which made it possible to count the 3,200.)

"Sunday evening in the Christian Center church Paul's message was for believers. He spoke on intercessory prayer. After the message, Paul invited those who wanted to accept Christ to come forward; to everyone's amazement 150 people responded.

"The weekend celebration began Saturday morning with a two-hour session on marriage, based on the experiences of Paul and Linda's 59 years of matrimony. It was beautifully accepted and several people gave their hearts to the Lord after their presentation of how to have a victorious marriage.

"On Monday before Hermano Pablo and Linda left Cuenca, the wife of a restaurant owner gave her testimony. 'My husband attended every service beginning at 10 a.m. Saturday, and I can't believe the change in him now, because he isn't the same man I married!'

"This is just one example of the many testimonies resulting from the weekend evangelistic campaign. One hundred new people are attending Christian Center church, and many others attend evangelical churches in Cuenca. Daily new people continue to accept the Lord."

God continues to build His church.

Chapter 36
Nothing to Contribute

Paul counsels a discouraged woman.

Many years ago Paul was preaching in Toronto, Canada, in the great People's Church when Hope Smith and Laurie Price were the pastors. After a morning service, a group went to a restaurant to eat. As they walked along the sidewalk, Rev. Smith pointed to Sister Mulch, a stately, quiet, reserved elderly woman walking ahead of them. "She is why I am in the ministry today."

When Hope was young, he didn't know what to do with his life. Just as a kind mother would for her beloved son, Sister Mulch encouraged him to give his life to God. You see, he thought that God couldn't use him because of his condition as a cripple. But now he is her renowned pastor.

The strange thing about this is that the very evening before Sister Mulch had asked Paul to pray for her. "Please pray for me, Brother Finkenbinder, as I feel so valueless in God's service. I try to let my light shine before others, but I can't do anything and I feel so discouraged. I need your prayers."

Paul hurried ahead to walk beside Mrs. Mulch. "Sister Mulch, I thought you told me that you can't do anything, that you are discouraged because you can't contribute anything to God."

"That's right, Hermano Pablo." Tears welled up in her eyes.

"You are wrong. I just learned how you encouraged Brother Smith to go into the ministry when he was young. Now he is your pastor."

"Oh, Smith has been talking to you. That's nothing." She lowered her head. "I have nothing to contribute. I can't sing. I can't preach. I am not even a good personal witness. I come from a poor background and have not had the opportunity to educate myself like other people. Therefore, I have nothing to contribute. I am not useful to anyone. I have nothing that another person needs." She dabbed her eyes.

"Mrs. Mulch, a light doesn't do anything but shine. It doesn't go anywhere. It doesn't say anything. It doesn't sing or preach. It just shines. Light is nothing more than light. That is precisely what God wants of us—that we let our light shine.

"God calls some people for certain tasks, and when He calls we need to respond. However, everyone is a light in this world. We are light, and what is important is our smiles, our personalities, our love, and our friendly dispositions—that is useful to God.

"There are more than 4 billion [at that time] people in the world, and no two are alike. It is when we try to be like someone else that our problems begin.

"The kingdom of God is like a great mosaic, made up of millions of tiny stones, and no two are alike. They are all different in size, color, shape, or density, and in some way, each one is distinct. If you take one of those stones out of the mosaic, the whole picture is ruined.

"You are one of these stones and God needs you just as you are. Two things are indispensable: One, you are clean of heart—and Jesus is the one who cleanses us. The Scriptures tell us that the blood of Jesus cleanses us of sin. The hands of God can form a beautiful vase from the ugliest piece of clay.

"And two, we must be dedicated to the Lord. We must be willing to be obedient to Him. These two requirements of being cleansed and available are what God wants in us. He doesn't expect more from us than what we are.

"When we say that we have nothing to contribute, we are comparing our life with some other person. God doesn't want to make us like another person. He is interested in using us as we are."

Sister Mulch, like many people, never considered herself of any value.

Appreciate who you are. Love yourself. Look at your life through the eyes of Jesus, who sees you as a precious stone.

Only when we accept our true value can we be our maximum service for God. God appreciates you. God loves you. Don't refuse to give God your maximum potential of service. He needs you just like you are.

Chapter 37
Do Not Judge

Paul learned that one should not judge others.

Our friend Edna Harrison invited Paul and me to a Catholic charismatic gathering in Anaheim, California, during the charismatic movement in the final years of the twentieth century. We entered the Catholic Church with Edna and were obligated to occupy front seats because the place was completely full.

For a full hour a priest directed the recitation of the Rosary, with repetitions, standing and kneeling many times. In his heart, Paul questioned how repeating the Rosary could be considered charismatic.

When the priest finished the Mass, he raised his arms and encouraged the congregation. "Now that we have fulfilled our responsibility to the church, stand to your feet and praise the Lord."

The whole group of some 500 people stood and with arms raised high, joyously praised the Lord; many of them spoke in tongues as in a Pentecostal meeting.

Paul was confused and criticized the situation in his heart. Lord, there is something wrong here. One moment these people are formally repeating the Rosary to Mary, and then they change to praising God, a total contradiction of religion.

While Paul meditated with this dissimilar manner of adulation, he sensed that God asked him, "Paul, how much do you think you don't know about me?"

He contemplated the enormity of the divine Creator. God, You are infinite and I know very little about You.

"Then how much do you calculate these Catholics know about me?"

God, when You put it in those terms, we are almost on the same level.

Paul says he nearly jumped out of his seat with God's reply: "Paul, I don't condemn you for your lack of knowledge, and you should not censure them for what they don't know."

The admonition in Mathew 7:1-2 confirms what God revealed to Paul that day. *"Do not judge, or you too will be judged. For in the same way you judge others, you will be judged and with the same measure you use, it will be measured to you."*

Paul says, "This lesson on judging others was a powerful lesson that I never want to forget."

Chapter 38
The Other Side of Faith

The Bible declares that without faith
it is impossible to please God
(Heb. 11:6).

We have the tendency to equate faith with miracles such as divine healings, but faith is much more than helps and cures.

We see a great miracle and we say either the people who prayed or the person who received the miracle had tremendous faith, or "There's a person of faith."

However, the book of Hebrews describes faith like this: *"Faith is the substance of things hoped for, the evidence of things not seen"* (Heb.11:1 KJV).

It's important to take notice that "faith" operates in that area of the unknown, in the realm of incognizance when we don't have the answer, when we have not yet seen the miracle, when we cannot see what the future holds for us, when everything is black and gloomy, and when even hope seems to slip away from our fingers.

In other words, faith is our outlook of trust, hope, belief, peace, assurance, joyful expectation, and even happiness in the midst of the trial. We do not want to suffer trials, but trials offer us an opportunity to exercise our faith. And don't forget, "Without faith it is impossible to please God."

You remember, of course, the story of the apostles Paul and Silas in the Philippian jail (Acts 16). They had been whipped with the traditional Roman 40 lashes minus one. Their feet were placed in chains, and if this were not enough, they were imprisoned in the inner dungeon, where it was dark, cold, and wet.

What were Paul and Silas doing under those deplorable circumstances? They were singing! Singing praises of worship to God. In fact, their singing attracted the other prisoners. That Paul and Silas could sing at a time like this was the greater attraction than the songs themselves.

We look at their situation in retrospect and say, "Of course, they could sing. They were about to be liberated by an earthquake." The truth is Paul and Silas were not expecting an earthquake. Their songs of worship and praise were an acceptance of and even joy for the privilege of suffering for the cause of Christ.

Paul and Silas simply accepted their lot and sang with joy in the midst of their trial. Their surrender and acceptance of their lot would have been the same had the earthquake never occurred. I can imagine they were as surprised as anyone else when the earthquake tore down the doors and broke open their chains. They didn't try to escape but remained under the Philippian jailer until authorities allowed them to leave the city.

Thumbing down the eleventh chapter of Hebrews, we run across verse 6, which says, *"And without faith it is impossible to please God."* If it takes a trial, a problem, a difficult time to afford us the situation where that attitude of confidence and trust can be exercised, then we would have to agree that without the trial, without the dark side of life, without large deficit balances, without illnesses, without circumstances that place us in a position where trust in God is exercised, it is impossible to please Him.

What can we say to all this? We need to recognize the following:

I must thank God for problems, and trials, and for every conflict I suffer, because these experiences allow me the opportunity to exercise faith. It is important to have faith in God, because it is through the trials, conflicts, confusions, and dark moments in our lives that we exercise our faith. When we have faith, we please God.

This is the other side of faith.

Chapter 39
Personal Convictions

"Every decision I make, I do it thinking of the result
of that decision 20 years from now."
—Paul Finkenbinder

One afternoon, I answered our home telephone. I placed the handset on the table and fairly ran to find Paul. My throat was tight with excitement. "Hon, it's the White House calling for you!"

Astonished that anybody in the White House of the United States of America knew his name, Paul took the phone. "Hello?"

The voice on the other end stated his name and the organization he represented, saying that he was inviting Paul to the White House for a meeting with Christian leaders of Latin American countries.

Surprised and at the same time elated, he thanked the person presenting this honor. But Paul had one question. "Will the press be there?"

"Oh, yes," the answer came confidently. No doubt the man believed Paul would definitely be more interested because of their presence.

"Then I cannot accept this kind invitation, because my picture and presence in the White House of the United States of America would prejudice my ministry throughout the Spanish world."

Paul was always concerned for the unbeliever's impression of his actions.

Paul's anxiety has always been if someone hears him preach the gospel of Jesus Christ but does not accept Jesus, it is because he was a bad example.

One day Paul offended a police officer in San Salvador as he directed traffic from a box in the center of an intersection. A shoulder of the directing officer meant one could continue driving, but if the officer faced the driver or gave his back, the driver needed to stop. Nearing the corner, Paul prepared to stop, but the officer started turning from his back to obviously give his shoulder, so he took the foot off the brake and drove on through.

Immediately, the shrill whistle of the traffic cop caught Paul's attention. So he dutifully pulled the automobile over to the curb and parked.

The ill-tempered officer complained that Paul didn't obey his signal.

Paul smiled and simply explained, "I began to stop and then you turned your shoulder, so I drove on through."

The infuriated official countered. "But you didn't wait until I completed my turn, because I turned all the way around."

"Then you deliberately tricked me, officer, because I logically believed you were turning to give me your shoulder."

The irate officer gave Paul two fines: One for violating his body signal, and the other for arguing with him.

Paul had to appear before a judge to answer the two charges.

After listening to Paul's explanation, the judge rendered his sentence. "I believe you. I will tear up the fines."

The next day Paul sought the young police officer. He went back to the same intersection, but he was not standing on his box at the same corner, so Paul drove the streets of San Salvador all morning until he found him. Paul parked his car, strolled up to the traffic officer, and asked, "Do you remember me?"

"Of course, I remember you." There was no mistaking the scorn in the officer's voice. "Did you pay the fines?"

"Yes, I took care of the fines, officer. I came to apologize for arguing with you yesterday. Because you represent the law, it was wrong of me to dispute your word."

The police officer was obviously taken aback. His demeanor softened. "No, I should apologize to you, for it was the end of the day and I was tired. I was rude to you."

Paul shook hands with the officer, parting as friends, with a clear conscience. He knew that if the police officer ever heard him preach, he would not reject the gospel because he had argued with him.

Paul always says, "My personal reputation is the most significant legacy I can leave the world."

Sure of his call to serve Christ, Paul was never tempted by offers of material benefits. Besides, he always took advantage of every opportunity to testify of the peace that only Jesus can give.

In 1954, Paul was in Salem, Oregon, for a missions convention. One afternoon while strolling through the town, he heard live music coming from a music store. He entered, listened a few moments to the man playing an organ, and then, because he can play by ear, Paul dared to put his hands on the upper keys of the organ and accompanied the man as he played.

The organist gave Paul a surprised glance, but he continued playing. When he finished that song, they played another number together. Then he suggested, "Let's play some songs together with you sitting at that organ." He pointed to another electronic instrument. They played several old-time numbers together.

After a few numbers, the organist walked over to Paul. "My name is Joe. Who are you and what do you do?"

Paul gave Joe his full name, explaining he was a missionary in El Salvador with his wife and family.

Joe smirked, as though he thought Paul was throwing his life away. "I'm searching for a person who can sit at an organ and play like you do. I'm in a position to offer you a monthly salary of"—and he named the figure, which was three times his missionary salary—"plus commission on organs that you sell."

Paul listened attentively to this sales clerk's attractive offer, looking for a way to tell him that he possessed something much more valuable. Finally, when Joe concluded his sale's pitch, Paul smiled. "And what else can you offer me, Joe?"

A look of surprise covered Joe's face. "And what else could you want?"

Paul looked straight into Joe's questioning face. "I am the happiest and most contented and satisfied man on earth. If you can guarantee me, Joe, the deep inner peace I now have, plus the liberal salary and the extra commissions, your offer would be a temptation."

Joe's expression turned solemn. "Paul, it appears you possess something far greater than my offer, and I want to hear about this peace you have. Let's eat lunch together."

Over sandwiches and coffee, Paul talked about the inner peace that only Christ offers humankind, and how this peace is available to everyone who will believe in Him. Joe listened intently and seemed genuinely interested. As they parted, Paul recommended that when he went to his hotel room that night (he was an itinerant salesperson) he should kneel down and invite Christ into his heart.

A few days later, Joe saw Paul in the street, and ran to him. Where before he was solemn, now he was excited. "I took your suggestion seriously and knelt beside my bed and prayed. I feel like an entirely different person!"

Said Paul, "It's true that I am the happiest and most contented and satisfied man on earth, and Joe recognized that what I had was what he needed to better his life."

Does Paul believe that he is divinely called of God?

"Perhaps in the biblical sense, God desires that I fulfill a certain plan. God chose Saul as the first king of Israel, and Saul was disobedient. In the same way, my call, or anyone's call, depends totally on obedience to God's call. It's our obedience, not our calls that determine our destinies."

When the apostle Paul, a perverse and violent man, persecuted the Christians, the Word of God says in Galatians 1:15-16, *"But when God, who set me apart from birth and called me by his grace, was pleased to reveal his Son in me so that I might preach him among the gentiles, I did not consult any man."*

According to the apostle Paul, God created each one of us, and He has a specific plan for each life.

One of Paul's interesting abilities is that he is never concerned about any question thrown at him. His ability to respond immediately is remarkable.

"Why don't you preach universal disarmament?" a loud-mouthed, anti-social university student in Santa Cruz, Bolivia, demanded of Hermano Pablo.

"Tell me, young man, have you ever seen a loaded gun go off by itself?"

"No, that couldn't happen." The student's volume lowered and his demeanor became sheepish.

"Of course not. And you never will observe a loaded gun discharge a bullet by itself," Hermano Pablo stated emphatically.

Turning to the entire group of university students, he explained, "The difficulty of the world is not the menacing gun; rather, the problem is the hostility in the human heart. We could bury every man-killing device—guns, rifles, and war machines—a mile deep in the ground, cover them with thick cement, and men will continue to murder with clubs and stones.

"The finger pulling the trigger is not at fault; rather, the evil in man's heart, motivating the finger to pull the trigger is the culprit."

Paul has a sixth sense and sees the scheme in the hearts of people who come to him.

A minister asked Paul to pray for him to receive the ministry gifts that Paul had.

"I don't know what you are talking about, but I will pray for you."

His prayer went something like this: "Lord, bless this brother, anoint him and use him in a mighty way. Give him all the gifts he needs, but never let him know he has them."

Paul believes that God's "called ones" are often limited in their activities for God by their selfishness, greed, and pride.

God used Paul's inspiration to send a missionary to Africa.

In 1966 Paul was the main speaker at the Assemblies of God campground service in Kalispell, Montana, near the magnificent Glacier National Park.

The superintendent of that district was reminding the churches to be faithful in giving financial help to a young missionary appointee Mary Ballenger, who was raising her support to go to Africa. He spent several minutes admonishing and encouraging people to pray and open their hearts to her need.

Suddenly Paul jumped to his feet, asked permission of the superintendent to address the congregation. "Friends, we aren't supposed to pray that Mary will get to Africa. God is in heaven. It isn't His responsibility to get Mary to Africa. The money to get her there is on this earth. It's our responsibility. If Mary goes to Africa it will be because we sent her there."

Within minutes, Mary's entire support was raised for her mission to Africa, where she still successfully ministers.

Testifying for Christ without words is Paul's preferential treatment of unknown people.

Paul went one afternoon to a local place in San Salvador to have a metal piece made for the car. He stood patiently in front of the mechanic who was working on another project. Finally, the man raised his eyes and impatiently barked, "What do you want?"

Paul explained his need. During the conversation, Paul noted that the mechanic was obviously aggravated. With love and compassion, he remarked, "It seems that you are having problems."

The attitude of the mechanic changed completely as he related difficulties he was having with his children. He seemed genuinely touched at Paul's interest in him.

The man smiled as Paul left and when he returned a few days later for the item he ordered, the mechanic treated him like a friend.

Paul never told him who he was. He just put into practice the counsel he gives others: "One should demonstrate the love of Christ constantly, and when the situation requires it, do it with words."

Our friend Neco had a difficult time understanding the gift of God's love.

One day our Salvadoran friend Neco MacEntee came to Paul with his solution to one of his many questions. "Pablo, I know I have to live many lives, die, and return many times until I satisfy God's requirements."

"Neco, everything we have comes from God; He never trades our dealings for His response. You cannot earn the favor of God. God loves and saves us out of pure love. Tell me, Neco, according to your present calculations of your existence, how many times do you estimate you have returned to the earth?"

He sighed. "Oh, Pablo, I am just beginning."

Paul placed his hand on his friend's shoulder. "Neco, if you return millions of times, if that were possible, you could never satisfy God's requirements."

"Then what can a person do to meet God's holy requirements?"

"You can do absolutely nothing to earn Christ's favor. Christ voluntarily paid the price for us, dying on the cross, making it easy to reach Him."

Neco scratched his head, deliberating. "I guess you can call it the difficult capability."

"Exactly Neco, it is impossible to put a price on the pure love of God."

All that God requires of us is that we accept Him as our personal Savior and that we maintain an intimate relationship with Him.

Paul is not preoccupied with the ministerial success of other ministers.

A dear colleague, interested in the success of Paul's ministry, came to him one day with a concern. "Hermano Pablo, Luis Palau is getting ahead of you. He is preaching in England."

Occupied with his crusades in Latin America and the production of his radio and television programs, Paul responded without irritation or jealousy. "Don't you know that Luis and I belong to the same team?"

"The success of Luis Palau or any other servant of God who preaches the gospel of Jesus Christ, are also my successes."

Chapter 40
Questions Reporters Ask — Testimonies

Paul followed the newspaper reporter to his car in Monterrey, Mexico, answering the customary questioning about ministry, what he was doing in the city, how many years he had been an evangelist, and the most frequently asked question, why does he use the name Hermano Pablo?

"Because my name is Paul Edwin Finkenbinder Argetsinger, and my radio program is only four minutes long." This forthright declaration regarding his outlandish-sounding German name to a Hispanic couldn't help but make the reporter smile. He continued with other questions.

The Mexican newspaper journalist wanted an interview before an evening service. Paul dislikes giving interviews just before his crusade message, but the brethren felt this could be important newspaper coverage to announce the services, so he agreed.

All reporters come prepared with a barb question that they pose unexpectedly, but Paul faces them confidently knowing that God will give him an answer to their questions.

The reporter slyly but sarcastically demanded an answer to his question "If your God is a deity of love, why is there so much war in the world?"

Instantly, Paul astonished the reporter with another question. "Have you ever had disagreements with your wife?"

"Of course, Hermano Pablo, who hasn't?"

"Tell me, who is in the wrong when you dispute: you or your wife?"

"My wife, of course," he promptly responded, indicating irritation at Paul's inquiry.

"So you are telling me that when it's a fight in the home, it's a human error, but in war with nations, which is nothing more than an extended fight of individuals, it's God's fault."

The exasperated reporter made no response, although the interview, including Paul's questions, made the newspaper.

"Hermano Pablo, doesn't it bother you that there are so many Catholics in Latin America and so few Protestants?" This reporter's critical question came during a live radio interview in Mexico City.

"No," Paul immediately exclaimed, "not in the least, sir. However, I am deeply concerned there are so many sad, dissatisfied people versus the few truly happy people. Enlighten me, sir, are you among the gloomy, disgruntled populace or the happy satisfied inhabitants?"

The interviewer immediately evaded the question, ending the interview with "I'm the one asking the questions."

Paul visited with President Suazo Cordova of Tegucigalpa, Honduras, in his private office and most courteously posed with

Paul so that I could take their picture together. As we left President Cordova's headquarters, a swarm of reporters surrounded Paul. One question that made the newspaper came from a sarcastic reporter who asked his question with a sneer. "Hermano Pablo, do you have the answer to the problems of the world?"

"I most definitely do," Paul responded confidently.

"What is it? Intellectuals, scientists, influential world leaders unsuccessfully seek solutions to the world's problems, and you claim to have it." Ridicule filled his voice.

"I'm not answering your question," Hermano Pablo responded bluntly, "because you are sarcastic and not sincere."

Other journalists crowded around Paul, insisting he inform them of the explanation of humanity's problems.

"The answer to the world's problems is for every individual to give his or her heart to God, for He alone is the author of peace."

Then the reporters asked another caustic question. "Hermano Pablo, are you a rightist or a leftist?"

Paul resented the question. "That is a trap question. According to your view, if I'm a rightist, I must hate all leftists; and if I am a leftist, I must hate all rightists. Perhaps this is your attitude, but I don't want to hate anyone."

TESTIMONIES

Dear Hermano Pablo,

Thousands of holes were drilled into the rock and into these holes thousands of sticks of dynamite were cautiously placed, discharging simultaneously at a given moment. The enormous dynamite explosion shook the ground and released the first layer of tons of rock. This drilling dynamite explosion repeated over and over again, removing rock until the mountain of rock was cleared away to form the enormous New York Harbor.

Hermano Pablo, that's what your message does as it finds its way deep into our spiritual lives and then disintegrates the obstacles that stand in the way of our spiritual growth.

Sincerely,
Jorge M. Broden-Arequipa, Peru - Nov. 1986

Hermano Pablo,

I greet you not as a friend but as your brother in Christ.

I want you to know the day your cassette arrived and I listened to "The plan of God for you", was the happiest day of my life.

I felt something special and began to cry, without realizing it, I raised my hands toward heaven, and I gave my life to Jesus Christ. My concerned wife called for the pastor of a nearby church to come and pray for me. That evening the pastor reported the testimony of the change in my life, and five of the band of drug dealers of which I was a member, gave their hearts to Christ.

Now we are praying for the remaining five members of this drug gang that they will also be won to the Lord. I beg for your prayers, Hermano Pablo, for six new believers in Christ and dismiss myself as your new brother in Christ.

Juan Venancio Arteaga
Santa Ana, El Salvador

Hermano Pablo,

Let me call you brother because, in reality, you are my brother even though we have different nationalities and different color skin—because we are both sons of God.

I am writing to tell you that your messages are little jewels that change the consciences of many people. I am slowly assimilating your messages that impact my heart in a profound way. One of your messages was about a smuggler. One day it occurred to this young man to swallow small diamonds and carry them undetected to another place. What he didn't realize was diamonds are glass and these diamonds cut through the walls of his stomach, and this man died an agonizing death. You concluded your message saying that many people, like that young man, are dying because they allow things like resentment, hatred, and bitterness in their hearts. Our happiness, you emphasized, is limited because of the sinful attitudes we carry inside us.

Hermano Pablo, I am so thankful to God for giving me the opportunity to hear your programs that teach me a little more every day. I almost forgot to tell you that I am a radio announcer and have the great privilege of putting your program on the air on Radio Centro here in San Juan, Dominican Republic.

Roberto Paulino

One Sunday in an afternoon church service in Los Angeles a man asked permission to say a few words and gave this moving testimony.

"I am Ernesto Vargas from Bolivia (and) a product of your ministry, Hermano Pablo. I was an active member of a militant Marxist group in Tarja, Bolivia, blinded by erroneous ideas. I belonged to a well-educated family, traveled, studied abroad, confident that communism is the only answer for the world and determined to do my part to eradicate opposing, especially religious, radicals.

"I was studying at the University in the years 1967-69 and in the evenings, I often frequented a small restaurant managed by Baptist believers. The restaurant kept the radio tuned to La Cruz del Sur, a Christian station, so everyone had to listen to your program, which I tried to ignore but could not. Every day your imposing program listened to by multitudes came on and one day a single phrase of your message affected me, 'The decision has to be yours.'

"The words clung to me, haunting me day and night. It was all I could hear for days, until the conviction of that phrase drove me to search for God. I searched for a time in religions, but God wasn't in religion. Then finally in 1970 I found the source of peace while visiting a tiny country church.

"I finished my studies, taught literature in the University, and later became Director of the University. I am living in Rosemead, California, and am studying theology in a Nazarene College because I want to take the message of Christ to my people.

"Your daily messages are reaching millions of people, Hermano Pablo; thank you for reaching me."

Ernesto Vargas, January, 1977

Raul Monson, the director of programming of YSU, who suggested the name "A Message to the Conscience" for Paul's four-minute radio program, worked clandestinely with a terrorist radio station in El Salvador. When war broke out Raul fled to Mexico where he contracted AIDS. When the war ended, he returned to El Salvador.

Several years ago, while Paul ministered in a Baptist church of 3,000 members in San Salvador, someone advised him that a woman wanted to see him after the service. She was the daughter of Raul Monson, who wanted to tell Hermano Pablo that her father had accepted Christ before he died. Our prayer for him for years had been that his own voice announcing the program would remind him of his need of Christ.

Chapter 41
Divine Healings

These marvelous healings beyond doubt are interventions by the God who says, "I am the LORD that healeth thee" (Exodus 15:26 (KJV)).

Deliverance from Sinus Allergy
San Salvador, 1952

Paul groaned and breathed heavily; his eyes watered. A hostage of endless Salvadoran dust, Paul also had constant pain in both ears. To make matters worse, the customary six months of tropical rains had ended in November, so enormous trade winds swirled smothering clouds of dust and debris under the doors and through the wood shuttered windows of our home.

Paul had experienced sinus pain all his adult life. This November morning he awoke with the worst throbbing headache imaginable. It was as though someone was jabbing pencils in both ears. Adding to his wretchedness, that evening he had to speak at a fellowship meeting in our local church in San Salvador.

At noon Paul informed the church pastor, Julio Rodriguez, of his illness and requested prayer. Julio and two other pastors came to our home and prayed for him. However, because of the unrelenting pain, Julio told Paul not to be concerned for the evening service because he would find another speaker.

Paul remained troubled regarding his speaking engagement. The terrible unremitting pain put him in anxiety. He sent again in the late afternoon for Pastor Julio, who arrived with two other colleagues. They anointed Paul with oil according to God's Word, quoted Scriptures, and claimed God's promises for his healing. Immediately, Paul sat up in bed. He told Julio to begin the church service and that he would be there to speak.

I protested as Paul staggered to his dresser for clothing, leaning against the wall as he shaved. I thought, "How can he speak when he is barely able to stand?"

Determined, although weak in body, Paul drove the few blocks to the church. He had wrapped a towel around his head because the ruthless swirling wind caused even more pain to his tender ears. At church, without the towel, he walked weakly to the podium. As he spoke, he felt renewed strength and became unconscious of pain. When the sermon ended, he realized all pain was gone!

The pain Paul had suffered all his adult life disappeared. Half a century later the marvelous healing of his sinuses still holds. To God be ALL the glory.

Diverticulitis
California, 1970

Paul cowered in a fetal position on the carpeted floor of the doctor's office, agonized with pain of another attack of some unknown source.

Full of compassion, the doctor looked down at him. "Paul you have diverticulitis. I'm sending you to the hospital immediately. You have damaged your body with the harmful spicy foods you eat. The only solution is immediate surgery."

Paul had suffered severe and frequent attacks for several years while ministering in his crusade trips to Latin America. Recently while driving alone in Costa Mesa, he had to park his car and sit bent over in his vehicle until an especially acute attack subsided.

Feeling weak and nauseous, Paul allowed me to drive him to the hospital, where he spent a miserable night fighting the thought of surgery. All night he mentally debated his alternatives for a healthy body without surgery.

Paul knew that the perfect solution for his distressing condition was to have faith in God for healing, which he desired but didn't have. The second alternative he contemplated was to have the dreaded surgery, but this did not appeal to him. The third, and final, option was to supervise his diet—including not eating red meat, which takes a long time to digest —and allow his body to heal by itself. Finally, Paul decided to take control of his body, watch his diet, and free himself of this health problem.

Early the next morning when the assigned surgeon entered his room, Paul informed him that he had decided against the surgery. The surgeon was visibly furious.

Paul left the hospital determined that he would allow his body to heal naturally by not eating foods that irritated his stomach.

Paul says, "I've had complete deliverance from the dreadful diverticulitis attacks because of using the wisdom God has given me."

Near Death Experience
California, 1989

In 1989, Paul ministered in La Paz, Bolivia, with Norm Mydske of the Billy Graham Association in a combination Congress on Evangelism and crusade services. Fred Cancio, his crusade soloist, accompanied him. Many times while he spoke, Paul used oxygen because of the 11,000-foot altitude. In the five days we were in that city numerous individuals accepted Jesus Christ as their personal Savior.

When the crusade ended, Paul desired a specific store item. An acquaintance walked with him and assured him the warehouse he needed was only three blocks away. Afterward we learned that the estimated distance to wherever you wanted to go was always three blocks.

A couple hours later Paul stumbled into our hotel room exhausted, frightfully pale, and barely making it to the bed before he collapsed. He asked me for peanuts to eat. I reluctantly gave him the peanuts, thinking that in his weakened condition the nuts were unhealthy for him. Later I learned that they probably saved his life because of the nutrients they contain.

The anticipated three blocks was actually more than 10 blocks of up-and-down hilly streets in that high altitude. And when he got to the store, Paul discovered that the item he wanted was not available.

That same evening, Eastern Airlines announced it had discontinued flying, so we needed to make other arrangements for our return to California. We chose the VARIG airline for our return—a grand airline that took us east and then north to California, an extremely tiresome 17-hour trip.

In Los Angeles Fred Cancio's sound equipment plus our combined luggage filled a large airport cart. Paul and Fred were pushing it up the long ramp to the upper floor. Cookie, Fred's wife, and I protested; we insisted they hire someone, because their health was more important than the few dollars it would cost. The fatigued but determined men continued pushing until they finally reached the street to Fred's son's waiting van. We then made the hour drive home to Costa Mesa.

The next day was Sunday. Paul and I occupied our customary seats at Newport Mesa Church, where we served as prayer leaders—praying with people who came forward for prayer.

Paul, unusually pale, turned to me and whispered, "Hon, I don't feel well enough to go forward to pray for others."

He appeared ill. I glanced toward the altar, seeking the attention of a prayer partner to pray for Paul. A woman saw me and came down the aisle to where we were seated. She prayed earnestly for Paul and then returned to her place at the altar.

Moments later Paul turned to me again. He said that he was terribly nauseated and unwell; he said he would wait for me in the car. (His mother was visiting us, so he asked me to remain with her.) As he walked toward the back of the church, the same woman who had prayed for him, and was providentially a registered nurse, felt unusually impressed to follow him. In the vestibule, she asked if he wanted to sit down.

"No, I want to lie down," and almost ran to a side room, where he fell to the floor, vomiting and almost passing out.

Someone immediately dialed 911; another came into the service to advise me of the situation. I knelt by Paul's head, frightened although not yet conscious of the seriousness of his condition. I began quoting from memory Psalm 91. I gained confidence in God and in His power while facing real terror as the paramedics took Paul's vital signs and glanced apprehensively at each other. Paul remembers hearing the paramedics stating his seriously low vital signs.

I repeatedly quoted, *"Because he loves me, says the LORD, I will rescue him; I will protect him, for he acknowledges my Name. He will call upon me, and I will answer him; I will be with him in trouble, I will deliver him and honor him. With long life, will I satisfy him and show him my salvation" (Ps. 91:14-16).*

Paul spent three days in the hospital. He received excruciatingly painful injections of potassium, the element needed to keep his heart pumping. It almost stopped beating because of the strenuous physical activities he'd endured, which depleted his potassium: the lengthy walk in the high altitude in Bolivia, the extended plane ride, and pushing the heavy luggage cart. Fortunately, we had peanuts in our room in Bolivia, and mercifully, God directed a registered nurse to follow Paul and get him the medical help he needed.

Undoubtedly, God has protected Paul because there are still many more Hispanic people who need the knowledge of salvation through Jesus Christ.

Diagnosis: Cancer
California, February 1998

Paul, with Norman Mydske, enjoyed four marvelous crusades in Piura, Arequipa, Pucallpa, and Iquitos, Peru.

It was an extremely hot arduous trip. We returned completely drained of strength, yet at the same time rejoicing at the goodness of the Lord. We usually recuperate physically within days, but after three weeks Paul was still exhausted and losing weight, so I insisted he see our doctor.

After several tests, our physician called to report that Paul had colon cancer and needed immediate surgery. I felt sick when I heard the report, but Paul calmly proclaimed in a loud voice, "My life belongs to God, and I am secure knowing He is in control of everything that happens to me. I know the God who did such marvelous miracles in people's lives in Peru can care for a simple thing like colon cancer."

Surgery was performed in April 1988; the cancer was small, completely contained, which made chemotherapy or radiation treatments unnecessary. The Jewish surgeon, conscious of Paul's faith in God, expressed, "Somebody upstairs is looking out for you, because the symptoms prompting you to see your doctor had nothing to do with cancer."

Paul, glorifying the Lord of heaven, says, "God has healed me many times because there are more cities to visit, more messages to preach, and more souls to rescue from an eternal hell."

Diagnosis: Leukemia
Irvine, California, 2010

Early Sunday morning of February 7, Paul awoke with severe chest pains. Paramedics rushed him to the hospital, where medical tests revealed that his chest pain was not caused by his heart but by pneumonia. After treatment for that, they kept him in the hospital for five days, seeking the cause of his high white cell count, which had escalated to 27,000. His blood and every part of his body tested well, so they took a bone marrow test, which indicated an infection in the leukemia family. Paul continued to be very weak, almost bedridden, eating very little, causing us to fear for his earthly life.

On Wednesday, March 3, after nearly a month of living in his pajamas, Paul awoke at 5 a.m. with the sensation that he was healed. An appointment that same day with the oncologist confirmed that his infection was not at the leukemia stage, stating that his extreme weakness could be caused by side effects of other medications. These have been modified and since that day God has manifested His power in giving Paul renewed strength and vitality. The white cell count went down to 19,000 and two weeks later to 9,000, which is normal.

Family and his myriad friends rejoice because God has touched Paul's body in answer to the many prayers in his behalf.

Chapter 42
A Successor for Hermano Pablo

"Every time I relate this miracle of passing my ministry to
Charles Stewart, my heart is newly inspired to trust
the God who has guided me and provided
for the future of this ministry."
—Paul Finkenbinder, also known as "Hermano Pablo"

"From the first radio transmission in 1955, God has been the owner of this work that surely would have failed if He Himself had not blessed and prospered my efforts to evangelize the Hispanic world," Paul affirms.

Friends inquisitively question his uppermost achievement in six decades of ministry. It is a difficult question to answer after a lifetime of following open doors leading to radio, television, films, crusades, and more.

"I guess if I had to choose one victory," Paul says, "it would be the unbelievable miracle that no human could have orchestrated the uniting of Charles and me and our two ministries." It is a marvel how Paul acknowledged Charles as his ministry successor, and Charles accepted all the responsibilities of Hermano Pablo Ministries.

At age 74, Paul was still managing Hermano Pablo Ministries, in addition to traveling 100 days of the year in crusades.

He worked hard writing the program anecdotes representing the depravities of man—fraud, alcoholism, infidelity, abortion, sexual depravity—and ending always with words of hope for the radio listeners and television viewers. For more than four decades, he faithfully prepared and recorded a daily Hispanic radio program of a loving God who longed to free people of their addictions. The arduous schedule was physically exhausting, but he never contemplated giving up.

His responsibilities included raising support for his evangelistic ministry to the Hispanic world—something categorically not his vocation. How this nonprofit organization known as Hermano Pablo Ministries, with 2,400 daily radio, television, and print releases (in 1996) of "A Message to the Conscience" succeeded during all those years, clearly and undeniably demonstrates the miraculous power of God.

In addition to his now-weary mind and body was the question of how to replace the old worn-out equipment with expensive television cameras and other necessary filming paraphernalia.

The Hispanic people who learned of the gospel of Christ did not financially support the ministry, so presenting the economic need to our friends who mostly did not know Spanish was his constant challenge.

These three burdens—making daily programs, purchasing new equipment, and marketing the ministry—became increasingly difficult for Paul. However, discontinuing the broadcasts would mean committing spiritual homicide of the myriad listeners waiting for the next day's message.

In January 1995, Paul and I ministered in the Josue Church in San Salvador, which our initial efforts in the 1960s had contributed to its birth. We unburdened our hearts of our advancing age and the ministry needs to the pastor, Rev. Lizandro Bojórquez, and asked him for advice and prayer.

We'll never forget his gentleness—taking both our hands in his and praying to God so quietly that his words were undistinguishable. But the prayer brought deep peace to our hearts.

The next day we flew home to Costa Mesa, California. Before we even reached our home—while still in the car of Jon and our daughter Bonnie—the answer to our prayer began. Bonnie handed us a letter from an anonymous donor who was giving Hermano Pablo Ministries $150,000 designated specifically for equipment, not for the running expenses of the ministry.

We comprehended immediately that God intended the permanency of Hermano Pablo Ministries, even though our personal involvement remained uncertain.

Later, in a ministry board meeting, Paul mentioned the subject of a successor, expressing faith in God's promise to provide someone for the continuance of the ministry. One of the men suggested that Paul call board member John Bueno, director of the Assemblies of God missionary department. Paul phoned our missionary colleague of El Salvador days. "John, I'm approaching 75 years of age, and since I can't live forever, I need somebody to pick up my mantle."

John interrupted the friendly conversation. "Paul, I already have him!"

"That's impossible, John. How could you possibly have somebody to succeed me when you didn't even know I was going to call you?" But before John could answer, Paul became curious, then excited. "Who is he?"

"His name is Charles Stewart, son of missionaries Verlin and Pauline Stewart, who served in Cuba for seven years before transferring to Colombia in 1960 when Castro took over.

"Charles Ray received his bachelor's degree in Missions, then pursued another bachelor's degree in Spanish literature, and ended up getting a master's degree in Latin American History.

He lives in Miami, is the Spanish Editorial Director of Life Publishers, and is a member of the committee translating the Bible into the Spanish NIV Bible.

"You can see, Paul, that he is well qualified. Charles has sent me scripts of proposed radio programs very similar to your "A Message to the Conscience" programs and asked my permission to begin a radio ministry."

Paul immediately sensed an awareness of another open door before him. "Would you call Charles and ask him to phone me this afternoon?"

At lunch that noon, Paul shared with me his conversation with John; we both sensed God was answering our prayers for a successor to Hermano Pablo Ministries. Our first concerns always are God's red or even yellow lights indicating watchfulness. But strangely, both Paul and I sensed complete tranquility. We had total confidence in the sovereignty of God and His guidance in our decisions.

Right there in our dining room we articulated fervent prayers for God's guidance. Relying totally on the direction of the Holy Spirit regarding the future, Paul returned to the office, eagerly waiting for Charles's phone call.

Charles called. The 90-minute conversation with Paul resulted in Charles accepting charge of Hermano Pablo Ministries and Paul's approving Charles as his successor in the ministry. You can imagine the conversation and the enthusiasm they shared as they compared their philosophies and their mutual burden to evangelize Latin America.

When Paul told the office staff that he had accepted Charles as the successor to the ministry, they looked at him in stunned silence; they wondered how he could have accepted him sight unseen—by only a phone call.

Everyone who hears this story of Paul's faith marvels. Paul cannot give a satisfactory explanation apart from the encompassing tranquility of God he sensed in his heart while conversing with Charles.

"I learned 50 years ago while attending Zion Bible Institute to rely on the Holy Spirit's guidance, and God provided a successor, as Linda and I believed He would."

Charles came to our office in Costa Mesa a few weeks later, met the staff and Hermano Pablo's Executive Board members, who readily voiced their approval of him. During the next year, Charles made frequent trips to California to record his "Message to the Conscience" programs that were intermingled weekly with Paul's already-taped programs. Since radio and television stations donate some $57 million of free time annually to Hermano Pablo, the integration of Charles's programs were carefully planned.

In July 1996, Charles, his wife, Linda, and family of five children moved to California to take over the ministry. Before they arrived, Paul and I took off in our motor home for two months, allowing the Stewarts an opportunity to establish themselves in the office without our intrusion.

Before beginning our travels, Paul admonished our office personnel not to expect another Hermano Pablo. The employees should realize that Charles was a different person, who would obviously do things his own way; he said they were to follow his leading because he was now in charge.

Paul called the office often, ascertaining everything was under control and assuring Charles of his delight in having him as God's provision for Hermano Pablo Ministries.

When we returned home from our motor-home trip in September, Paul and I believed we were mentally prepared for the necessary changes in our office; however, we never anticipated the emotional impact upon seeing our personal offices that had been ours for 28 years now belonging to Charles and Linda Stewart. Our office photos and documents were replaced with their plaques and pictures, while ours neatly adorned the walls of the halls and conference room.

For a few brief moments, Paul and I silently observed the office changes and the end of the latest epoch in our lives. At the same time we savored vivid reminiscences of the past 50 years.

A diversity of emotions stirred within us as we said our farewells and hurried to our car, where I slumped in the seat. "Hon, I feel so nauseated."

Paul, ever optimistic, admitted dismally, "I know, Hon. This office isn't ours anymore, and I feel sick to my stomach too. But let's thank God for sending the Stewarts, relieving us of responsibilities and giving permanency to Hermano Pablo Ministries."

Our praises brought quietness and peace to our emotions. Even before starting the car, our prayers brought healing of the traumatic pain in the pit of our stomachs that we never permitted to surface again.

Paul jubilantly proclaims, "Faith and confidence in God's sovereign ability to guide by His Holy Spirit permitted me the joy of experiencing this marvelous God-ordained miracle."

Chapter 43

Hermano Pablo Today

*The ambitious youth who consecrated his heart and life to God,
wanting to be a missionary, became frustrated at not reaching
the masses from the back of a mule. Without funds or
equipment, he signed radio and television contracts
to evangelize El Salvador. These efforts surely would have
failed if God had not been in them.*

Paul received his license to preach from the Latin American District of the Assemblies of God September 9, 1942. On March 23, 1948, while ministering in El Salvador, he received his credential of ordination from the Assemblies of God headquarters in Springfield, Missouri.

On May 8, 1993, Vanguard University of Costa Mesa, California, issued Paul an honorary Doctor of Divinity award for his 55 years of faithful service.

Hermano Pablo, loved and honored by the Hispanic world, can now boast of almost 6,000 a day of his A Message to the Conscience® program by radio, television, or newsprint in 33 countries of the world. In addition, more than 50,000 people download his program daily from the Internet.

Paul is happy and self-confident. He never takes credit for his successes. Accolades are like "water off a duck's back."

Praise does not affect him. He does not need "amens" from an audience when he is speaking. He believes that if he lifts himself up, at some point in time he will fall flat on his face. On the other hand, if others lift him up, he does not need to fear.

Paul also never recognizes an enemy. "If someone doesn't like me that is his problem," he says.

One of Paul's outstanding character traits is that he is never jealous of other ministers and doesn't care who gets the credit. I remember well a recent special service in Lima, Peru, where they honored the ministry and life of Hermano Pablo. After the service, when we returned to our hotel, I asked him what he was thinking about during all the accolades they had showered on him.

Very solemnly he answered, "I was sad as I thought of the many ministers who labor faithfully for the Lord and never receive recognition for their efforts." Paul never believes himself better than others.

When Paul is speaking with someone, he always gives that person his full attention, looking directly at him or her and ignoring others around him. Sometimes someone has to tug his sleeve to remind him that others are waiting or that it is time to leave.

"Paul has a naïve and gullible quality about him—even stupid," one of his colleagues once said of him. "You can be rude to him, criticize him unfairly and he will not do anything to defend himself. He doesn't pretend to be knowledgeable, but he is all heart. He is liberal in paying his way, but is very rigid when he talks business. He is never underhanded in any way. Paul is a boy with a poor memory. He forgets everything. He is the boy who forgets that five minutes ago someone offended him. He never remembers the bad things. He always speaks victoriously. He is a mature man with the heart of a child."

Paul was 34 years of age when he started in radio. Now at almost 90, with long silvery white hair, he walks slowly with a cane because he could fall easily; he is deaf without hearing aids; and his memory is fading regarding details and incidents of the past.

Almost fanatically, Paul reads a certain number of chapters of the Bible daily. He loves God's Word, remains positive and confident of God's guidance and direction of his life. He never fears illness or calamities—knowing that God is in control of everything.

He is fascinated and entertained daily with the history of God's creation and of the beauties of the new heaven and new earth that God has prepared for us.

"My prayer," Paul says, "is that the history of my life inspires others to follow my example of faith and confidence in God's promises.

"Pick up the mantle that I am laying down, and continue the task that Jesus gave each one of us in Mark 16:15: *'Go into all the world and preach the gospel to all creation.'*"

Epilogue
Charles Rey Stewart's Radio Messages

A MESSAGE TO THE CONSCIENCE
by Charles Rey Stewart
29 March 2010

THE DONKEY AT THE TRIUMPHAL ENTRY

An interesting fable tells of the famous morning when Jesus entered Jerusalem seated on the back of a lowly donkey. When the donkey returned to his stable, all the other animals gathered around to find out all that had happened. The donkey began to swagger among his friends and, assuming a pretentious stance, told them, "You can't imagine how popular I was in the crowd this morning. Everyone ran to see me pass by, and no one allowed my fine hooves to be soiled with the dirt of the ground. They all threw their coats down so that I could walk over them.

A cow asked, "And when they threw their coats down so that you could pass, what did they say?" "Well," responded the donkey with even more pride, "they said, 'Hosanna! Blessed is he who comes in the Name of the Lord!'"

Upon hearing this, all the animals laughed uproariously. "What an idiot you are!" one of them said. "That honor wasn't for you. It was for the one you carried on your back. It was for Jesus, the Son of God."

Hermano Pablo recounted this fable on the radio three years after his first program, broadcast on July 1, 1955, which eventually became A MESSAGE TO THE CONSCIENCE. What is noteworthy is that after over fifty years of consecutive broadcasts in which programs have begun with similar stories, their author has not stopped identifying himself with the donkey of the fable.

Paul has not changed much since granting the first interview to George Grey of the Orange County Register in 1978. "Paul said he sees himself as a 'donkey' for God," Grey reported back then. "He recites the Biblical account of the donkey who carried Jesus Christ into Jerusalem." In Paul's own words:

> The donkey in a fable tells another donkey how important he is. He claims that as he entered Jerusalem the crowds of people threw flowers in his path that they hung garlands of flowers about his neck, and they smiled at him and cheered him.
>
> "In a sense we who serve . . . are like that donkey, and we must be careful to know that it is the message we carry, our rider so to speak, which is more important than we. I have that feeling in my ministry, that in a sense I am a donkey, carrying the word.

Clearly Hermano Pablo has a self-image that is totally the opposite of the following tribute to him that was published in the daily newspaper La República of San José, Costa Rica:

... Hermano Pablo... rejects the well-worn paths of religious oratory and becomes a dynamo that flips the switch of the unusual to turn on the light in the minds of his audience.

He is a "hammer" that strikes everyone's conscience, a counselor who does not resort to cheap demagoguery nor comes across like a saint, but rather with the status of a teacher . . .

... a voice proclaiming peace and love in a world filled with blood and violence...

It is refreshing to listen to him . . .

His words convey serene reflection and rational religious thinking.

. . . For this Hermano Pablo . . . whose voice is heard in all the Spanish-speaking world, is a man dedicated to Christ who has his feet firmly planted on the ground.

A MESSAGE TO THE CONSCIENCE
by Charles Rey Stewart
1 July 2010

55-YEAR ANNIVERSARY ON RADIO

On Friday, July 1, 1955, he recorded his first radio program on radio station YSU in San Salvador, El Salvador. That program, "The Church of the Airwaves," fifteen minutes in length, was broadcast Monday through Saturday for the next nine years. Then, in its place he created his popular four-minute program known worldwide as A MESSAGE TO THE CONSCIENCE®. It is none other than Paul Finkenbinder, known internationally as Hermano Pablo (Spanish for "Brother Paul"). In 2010, the year he celebrates his 55th anniversary on radio, this program (that thousands have listened to since they were children) is not only broadcast on radio but also on television and in print media, currently more than 5,800 times each day in 33 countries. So in the course of more than half a century of continuous media presence, it is no wonder that the voice of Hermano Pablo has become perhaps the most listened-to voice in all the Spanish-speaking world.

To what can we credit the success of this enduring presence in mass media? In great part, it is due to the integrity that characterizes Hermano Pablo and the love that emanates from him. For those of us who have had the pleasure of knowing him personally, there is no doubt that he is upright and modest, the same in a private conversation as in a public meeting, the same at home and in the office as on the radio and television. In other words, Hermano Pablo practices what he preaches. And when he preaches loving God and others, it's as if the love oozes out of his pores. The love that radiates from him, to the elite of society just as to those who are less influential, is a shining example for all to see.

Thus Dr. Pedro Rivero Mercado, director of the newspaper El Deber of Santa Cruz, Bolivia, wrote, "From the very first time I met Hermano Pablo, I was left with the impression that I had known him all my life." In the same vein, Sandra Maria Mora Chinchilla, from San José, Costa Rica, wrote to Hermano Pablo,

"The Lord knows how he will compensate you for your dedication and great love. I met you when you were visiting Costa Rica. I worked at the hotel where you came to stay, and I had the honor of checking you in to your room. What most amazed me was how sweet you were and the peace you seemed to have."

In short, it can be said of Hermano Pablo, without fear of contradiction, that throughout his life he has set the consummate example of following the commandments that Jesus chose as the most important: to love God with all your heart, and to love your neighbor as yourself.1 For that reason, we take advantage of this fifty-fifth anniversary on radio to express our appreciation to Hermano Pablo, just as Sandra Maria did in ending her letter, "Thank you for your help and for your total commitment."

A MESSAGE TO THE CONSCIENCE
by Charles Rey Stewart
2 July 2010

"WORDS OF FIRE, GOLD, AND SILK"

"It was a holiday when my youngest brother died of meningitis . . . in Puerto Rico, the land of my birth. That bitter day, like all the miserable days of my early childhood, the townspeople celebrated, indifferent to our pain. We searched for a carpenter to make the coffin, amid the sound of laughter. We didn't have any money, and the carpenter was nowhere to be found, so my father and I used some furniture and scrap lumber to make a rough coffin in which to lay our beloved little dead one. The next day, I, who had been going through a rebellious stage, far from Christ and from the problems of this world, promised God that I would serve Him."

That is how Hermano Pablo tells his "story of infinite sadness," according to a reporter from La Prensa Gráfica (newspaper in El Salvador) who interviewed him in 1971, upon his return to El Salvador where he had previously lived for twenty-one years. The promise that the boy made that day, to serve God, was fulfilled by Hermano Pablo like never before, on the first of July of 1955. That day, on radio station YSU in San Salvador, his first program was broadcast, and nine years later became A MESSAGE TO THE CONSCIENCE®.

Fifty-five years have come and gone since that first radio broadcast, and yet that Salvadoran journalist's judgment remains true when it comes to Hermano Pablo, whose "big brotherly smile" complements "his words of fire, gold, and silk." Here is his personal commentary about Hermano Pablo published in La Prensa Gráfica:

> "It is hardly necessary to describe the intellectual and human side of this pastor, for our people, along with the rest of the people of America, have become familiar with his [Hermano Pablo's] courageous, clear, vibrant, and human manner of expressing himself. Ambition, suffering, unhappiness, our unbalanced morals in this age of confusion, compassion, anxiety, all of the aspects pertaining to the human heart tortured by its base passions, find in the words of this shepherd the right angle, the clear focus, the suitable phrases, and the moral of the story that comes across as well-reasoned philosophy. Three minutes is all the

time this brilliant sacred orator needs to settle a matter from a human and philosophical perspective, and his approach squares perfectly with Biblical thought, which thereby takes on eternal relevance. The three minutes in which Hermano Pablo delivers A MESSAGE TO THE CONSCIENCE bring us ever closer to the admirable Christ of the Sermon on the Mount. In his words we hear Christ constantly repeating to us, "I am the resurrection. I am the way. I am the truth. Follow me!"

Photo Album

Pioneer Missionaries
Ralph and Jewel Williams with
Paul and Linda, 1943

Francisco Arbizu, Paul's (mule)
traveling companion

Paul first evangelized
on mule back

Paul's car destroyed by train

Rev. Gordon Lindsay starts paying
for station time in Honduras,
October 1955, initiating Hermano
Pablo's international radio ministry

Hermano Pablo when he started
radio broadcasting

The first radio studio in our garage

New converts

A new radio studio

Assembly of God leaders
in El Salvador
Seated: Francisco Arbizu.
Missionaries: Arthur Lindvall,
Paul Finkenbinder, Lois and David
Stewart

A live television program

A scene from The "Elijah and
Baal" movie

Soloist Fred Cancio blesses the crusade congregation

Rev. Norman Mydske, director of
Billy Graham Crusades, directed
Hermano Pablo Crusades
for 35 years

The people respond to an altar call

Hermano Pablo and Linda with
Fred and Cookie Cancio

Hermano Pablo, always with a
microphone

The Finkenbinder family, 1958

Seeking God's help

Hermano Pablo live on television
answers the questions
of the people

Billy Graham poses with
Hermano Pablo

Prominent evangelists in Latin
America: Alberto Mottesi, Luis
Palau, and Hermano Pablo

Reverend John Bueno,
Executive Director of Assemblies
of God World Missions

Carlos Rey Stewart and wife, Linda

Paul receives an honorary doctorate
from Vanguard University, 1993

The Finkenbinder family, 1992.
(From left: Paul R, Bonnie, Paul,
Ellin, Linda, Joanie and Gene)

Hermano Pablo
A gift from the Pardillo's
in Mexico City

Hermano Pablo with Carlos Rey,
new Director/President of Hermano
Pablo Ministries.

Headquarters of Hermano Pablo
Ministries in Costa Mesa,
California

Paul and Linda, 1942

Paul and Linda, 2008

CPSIA information can be obtained at www.ICGtesting.com
Printed in the USA
269239BV00005B/3/P